Teacher Preparation at the Intersection of Race and Poverty in Today's Schools

Teacher Preparation at the Intersection of Race and Poverty in Today's Schools

Edited by
Patrick M. Jenlink

ROWMAN & LITTLEFIELD
Lanham • Boulder • New York • London

Published by Rowman & Littlefield
An imprint of The Rowman & Littlefield Publishing Group, Inc.
4501 Forbes Boulevard, Suite 200, Lanham, Maryland 20706
www.rowman.com

6 Tinworth Street, London SE11 5AL

British Library Cataloguing in Publication Information Available

Library of Congress Cataloging-in-Publication Data Available

ISBN 978-1-60709-867-6 (cloth)
ISBN 978-1-60709-868-3 (pbk.)
ISBN 978-1-60709-869-0 (electronic)

Contents

Preface

The intersection of race and poverty is a not a new issue to America; rather, it is an issue that has a long and deep history. The Institute of Race and Poverty (IRP) in Minneapolis, Minnesota, was established in 1939 to identify and address problems caused when racial and economic discrimination combine to create barriers to opportunity for low-income communities of color. During its history, the IRP has focused on issues of race and poverty, often giving voice to the larger public on the tensions that exist in our society. Tensions of race and poverty predate the Civil War, were present during the civil rights movement, and are deeply woven into the fabric of our history, both societal and educational.

Today, we continue to face challenges at the intersection of race and poverty, perhaps most crucially in schools across America. Teacher educators, in preparing teachers to enter schools where the intersection of race and poverty is most prevalent, are confronted with the responsibility of ensuring that teachers understand what lies at the intersection of race and poverty and how it affects the lives of students and teachers alike as they engage in relationships of teaching and learning bound inseparably to past and present tensions of race and poverty.

The intersection of race and poverty in society and schools is a significant concern to our country, to our educational system, and to our preparation of teachers who must enter classrooms each day and meet the challenges that are presented. Importantly, the intersection of race and poverty exists in rural, suburban, and urban population centers.

The most dangerous place for a child to grow up is at the intersection of race and poverty, and the most challenging place for a teacher to teach is in schools where the intersection of race and poverty is woven into the fabric of students' lives. The work of teacher preparation, in large part, is to ensure that all children are educated both in terms of knowledge and understanding and in terms of life and the responsibilities of democratic citizenry. The teacher entering a classroom at the intersection of race and poverty is met with challenges of racial and economic inequality and slow erosion of the spirit and imagination of young minds growing up in racial and economic turmoil.

Teacher Preparation at the Intersection of Race and Poverty in Today's Schools is a collection of thoughtful works by authors who represent current thinking about teacher preparation. Importantly, the book is divided into two primary parts. The first four chapters offer an understanding of the depth and breadth of the intersection of race and poverty as it relates to teaching and teacher preparation. The second section presents dialogues of teacher education, focused on meeting the challenge. These eight contributing authors reflect on and give voice to meeting the challenge.

Part One

Introduction

Chapter One

Teaching at the Intersection of Race and Poverty in Today's Schools

Patrick M. Jenlink

While one of the most dangerous places for a child to grow up in the United States is at the intersection of poverty and race that defines their lives, one of the most challenging, and at times equally dangerous, places for a teacher to enter the classroom is also at the intersection of poverty and race. In the United States, White-Black race relations are systemic, as is poverty; both are reproduced culturally, institutionally, and socially from generation to generation with, all too often, no indication of systemic solutions forthcoming. This systemic racism and poverty confer a permanent minority status to the non-White that is ignored in contemporary treatments of race and poverty. Importantly, poverty confers a permanent minority status to "White" that is also ignored in contemporary treatments. [1]

Teachers in public school classrooms are confronted with the systemic nature of race and poverty, albeit with little or no preparation for how to address the problem, let alone how to work with students who do not see a future that is different from the conditions they presently experience. The concern for equality in treatments of race and poverty has a long history in the United States. Chief Justice Earl Warren's opinion in the historic case *Brown v. Board of Education* (1954) witnessed a step toward racial equality:

> [Education] is required in the performance of our most basic public responsibilities, even services in the armed forces. It is the very foundation of good citizenship. Today it is a principal instrument in awakening the child to cultural values, in preparing him [or her] for later professional training, and in

> helping him [or her] to adjust normally to his [or her] environment. In these
> days, it is doubtful that any child may reasonably be expected to succeed in life
> if he [or she] is denied the opportunity of an education. (p. 494)

The decision of the court was viewed as progress that gave integrated schools an equalizing, socializing, nationalizing—assimilationist and secular—mission (Bickel, 1978, p. 121); however education as a focal point of *Brown v. Board of Education*,[2] as Bickel (1978) noted, was a small step with historical significance.

Unfortunately, poverty in the United States has not witnessed a comparable Supreme Court decision to ease its systemic nature. That said, many would argue that while *Brown v. Board of Education* was a step forward, it has not proven to be the systemic solution for equality that race and racism require.[3] Milner and Laughter (2015) make an important point concerning poverty, a point that teachers need to understand.

> Poverty, in many ways, is socially constructed because there is diversity in
> people's experiences of living around or below the poverty line . . . from a
> philosophical perspective, we suggest that poverty is not an absolute term but a
> relative one that depends on a wide range of factors beyond yearly income,
> factors like wealth, occupation, income, education, power, and social status.
> (p. 353)[4]

American educational systems, both the public schools and postsecondary systems, have a long history of racial and socioeconomic segregation and inequality, which has persisted despite the 14th Amendment of the US Constitution, *Brown v. Board of Education* and its offspring, the passage of civil rights legislation, and the civil and human rights movements. Today, children in the United States continue to be segregated by race and socioeconomic status and attend schools that are not only separate but also grossly unequal in both resources and academic outcomes.

To understand what teaching in a democratic society and its schools and classrooms means, it is instructive to reflect on John Dewey's 1916 address calling for democratic nationalization of the US educational system. In his address, Dewey argued:

> Since our democracy means the substitution of equal opportunity for all for the
> old-world ideal of unequal opportunity of difference classes and the limitation
> of the individual by the class to which he [or she] belongs, to nationalize our
> education is to make the public school an energetic and willing instrument in

developing initiative, courage, power and personal ability in each individual. . . . So I appeal to the teacher . . . to remember that they above all others are
the consecrated servants of the democrat ideas in which alone this country is
truly a distinctive nation. (p. 428)

Given that Dewey's address spoke specifically to teachers, this call for action
should arguably be a consideration for teacher educators and for the very
nature of what teacher preparation programs are and/or should be in the
United States, as they are instrumental in shaping school cultures and cli-
mates, and in adopting and enacting a school's actions toward its students,
their families, and the communities in which they live, work, and play.

TEACHERS AT THE INTERSECTION

Teachers leaving university preparation programs and entering public school
classrooms find that the intersection of race[5] and poverty is a clear and
present problem for students and, in particular, for teachers who are not
prepared to meet the problem head-on of teaching students burdened by
inequality. The growing racial and socioeconomic isolation of schools in the
United States is mirrored by growing inequalities in funding. Equally a factor, "high-minority and high-poverty schools often also have the added bur-
den of lower levels of funding, lower teacher quality, and higher dropout
rates. The result is that students whose families already face hardship are
placed at an even greater disadvantage" (Leadership Conference Fund, 2013,
p. 7). Preparing teachers for growing inequalities in funding, high poverty
rates and higher dropout rates compounds the already problematic nature of
preparing teachers for the intersection of race and poverty in schools.

At the intersection of race and poverty, especially within the context of
urban and suburban centers like Baltimore, Charlottesville, Detroit, Ferguson, and other communities, attitudes toward "the establishment" and economic power may be as much, if not more, of a concern. Cindy Long (2017)
speaks to a clear and present concern for teachers to address that is evident in
the Charlottesville, Virginia,[6] event:

In the wake of the violence in Charlottesville, Virginia after one of the largest
white nationalist rallies in recent years, our kids are confused and scared. They
have more questions than ever, and parents and educators who are experiencing their own shock and disbelief are struggling to find the right words to offer.
(para. 1)

Preparing teachers to address the increasingly frequent events like that in Charlottesville is not the typical university curriculum; yet it has become a reality for teachers in classrooms across the United States.

Teacher preparation has a responsibility to focus on race and poverty, to focus on preparing teachers to enter classrooms and engage students in ways to mediate the tensions that students experience at the intersection of race and poverty. Teacher educators have a civic and social responsibility to prepare teachers who work with students coming from the race and poverty intersection so that these students see a future different from the past and present they experience. Classroom teachers need to focus on helping students become the people they are supposed to be, irrespective of where they are in the intersection of race and poverty. NEA president Lily Eskelsen García (2017) writes in her blog:

> It's not important that we, as adults, know all the answers. It's important that we let them ask all the questions and explore the complexity of our human family. And it's important that children know that there is right and there is wrong. (para. 6)

Teacher educators, in addressing the events that are defining our country, as in Charlottesville, are witnessing an unprecedented scenario of hate and racism[7] that draws public school teachers into uncharted territories. Addressing these events, along with with preparing teachers for the intersection of race and poverty that defines students, will prove to be difficult, yet necessary, challenges in teacher preparation. Ensuring that preservice teachers understand the importance of right and wrong, in particular as related to racism and poverty, and of providing a forum where students have an opportunity to speak and ask hard questions is quintessential.

As Milner and Laughter (2015) argue, good intentions are not enough; teacher preparation for the intersection of race and poverty needs to help teachers "understand and question why a disproportionate number of students of color live in poverty and are from lower socio-economic backgrounds if they want to provide a set of experiences for their P–12 students that allow them to build insights about inequity" (p. 345). It is important that, as teacher educators responsible for preparing the next generation of teachers, we do not ignore the intersection of race and poverty. Importantly, such teacher preparation needs to "acknowledge or talk about why and how it matters" (p. 345).

FINAL REFLECTIONS

As teacher educators, we should be concerned with people's perceptions of how race and poverty impact students, and how, in turn, race and poverty impact teaching and learning. It is these perceptions that are most in need of concern. As teacher educators, we need our students to be both race conscious and poverty conscious.[8] Important to teacher preparation is creating a pedagogical framework for understanding race and poverty to inform teacher preparation that is based on a comprehensive and critical set of ideas, which does not blame students from diverse racial origins or students in poverty for being non-White or poor or casts them as less equal; rather, we need teacher preparation to recognize the social, political, and economic conditions that have profound influences on the day-to-day lives of students who live at the intersection of race and poverty (Ullucci & Howard, 2015).

NOTES

1. Angela Glover Blackwell highlights the seriousness of the intersection of race and poverty: "Those of us working to end poverty and racism used to make our case in moral terms: the nation must deliver on the promise of equal opportunity and shared prosperity because it is the right thing to do. But a demographic transformation more rapid and widespread than anyone had predicted has changed the conversation. By the middle of this century, the very same groups who have long been left behind will become America's majority population. By the end of this decade, most youth will be people of color. These shifts already have occurred in California, Texas, New Mexico, and in metropolitan regions across the country. Equity—just and fair inclusion in a society in which all can participate and prosper—has become more than a moral issue. It is now an economic imperative" (n.d., para. 2).

2. The Leadership Conference Fund Report (2013) noted: "The promise of Brown v. Board of Education was a country in which students, regardless of race, would have an equal opportunity to learn. However, that promise remains unfulfilled: American students remain deeply divided by class and race, with, as before, racial minorities and low-income students far more likely to receive a substandard education and to be treated poorly" (p. 8).

3. Equality, in creating both the measure of humanity and the desire of non-Whites to be included into that humanity, can only be unveiled through non-White people's "surrender of their historical and culture orientation—their peoplehood" (Curry, 2008, p. 42).

4. Teachers need to be able to understand poverty as a fluid construct and to not stereotype their students and families based on quantitative indicators and metrics.

5. It is important for teachers to understand that "students have complex racial identities and these complex identities should be considered; yet, many teachers are allowed to complete their educational training without any or very few opportunities to really learn about race" (Milner & Laughter, 2015, p. 351).

6. The violence in Charlottesville, after one of the largest white nationalist rallies in recent years, spurred young James Fields to ram his car into a crowd of people standing up for racial justice, resulting in the death of Heather Heyer and the wounding of dozens more.

7. Tatum (2001) is instructive on the concern of racism in society and the importance of preparing teachers to enter the classroom: "In a race-conscious society, the development of a positive sense of racial/ethnic identity not based on assumed superiority or inferiority is an important task for both White people and people of color. The development of this positive identity is a lifelong process that often requires unlearning the misinformation and stereotypes we have internalized not only about others, but also about ourselves" (p. 53).

8. *Race conscious*, as Teel and Obidah's (2008) explain, refers to racially competent teachers having an "awareness of race, of the possibility of their own racism and the racism of others, and the significance of these perceptions in the teaching and learning process" (p. 4).

REFERENCES

Bickel, A. (1978). *The Supreme Court and the idea of progress*. New Haven, CT: Yale University Press.

Blackwell, A. G. (n.d.). America's tomorrow: Race, place, and the equity agenda. Retrieved from http://www.whatworksforamerica.org/ideas/americas-tomorrow-race-place-and-the-equity-agenda/#.W-Tm8-lRf-Y.

Brown v. Board of Education, 347 U.S. 483 (1954).

Curry, T. (2008). Saved by the Bell: Derrick Bell's racial realism as pedagogy. *Philosophical Studies in Education, 39*, 35–46.

Dewey, J. (1916). Nationalizing education. *Journal of Education, 84*(16), 425–28.

Garcia, L. E. (2017). *Lily's Blackboard*. Retrieved from http://lilysblackboard.org/2017/08/the-people-we-are-supposed-to-be/.

Leadership Conference Fund. (2013). *Still segregated: How race and poverty stymie the right to education*. Shadow Report of The Leadership Conference Education Fund, Washington, DC.

Long, C. (2017). Talking to students about Charlottesville violence and racism. Retrieved from http://neatoday.org/2017/08/14/talking-to-students-about-charlottesville-events/.

Milner, H. R., & Laughter, J. C. (2015). But good intentions are not enough: Preparing teachers to center race and poverty. *Urban Review, 47*, 341–63.

Tatum, B. D. (2001). Professional development: An important partner in antiracist teacher education. In S. H. King & L. A. Castenell (Eds.), *Racism and racial inequality: Implications for teacher education* (pp. 51–58). Washington, DC: AACTE Publications.

Teel, K., & Obidah, J. (2008). *Race in the urban classroom: Developing educators' cross-racial competence*. New York, NY: Teachers College Press.

Ullucci, K., & Howard, T. (2015). Pathologizing the poor: Implications for preparing teachers to work in high-poverty schools. *Urban Education, 50*(2), 170–93.

Chapter Two

Appropriation or Culturally Relevant Education?

The Place of Black Student Culture in School Curriculum

Kelly Wallace and J. Amos Hatch

The project described in this chapter grew out of both authors' feelings of intrigue over whether teachers should use elements of Black student culture as tools for teaching the academic curriculum. Like the vast majority of teachers in US public schools, we are both White, and we are particularly interested in the implications for White teachers when this question is taken seriously.

Kelly was a PhD candidate in English education, and Amos was a professor of urban-multicultural teacher education. Our engagement with this question began in a cross-department doctoral seminar, where Kelly led a discussion on issues raised in a review she had written (Wallace, 2016) of David Kirkland's (2013) *A Search Past Silence: The Literacy of Young Black Men.* The discussion between us continued during the summer and fall semesters following the seminar, and at some point, we decided to keep track of what we were saying, thinking, and finding in the literature in hopes that our explorations would be useful to others.

The interchanges that follow trace the steps we took during this sometimes awkward journey. The first entries introduce our perspectives, set the context, and sample some pertinent literature. The dialogue that follows is an edited version of tape-recorded conversations between us, supplemented with email correspondence and notes taken throughout the process. We have not found a definitive answer to the question of whether teachers are appropriating Black student culture when they attempt to teach content by making connections between the content and the culture, but we believe an exposition of our struggle with the sensitive issues involved will be useful to others who are reflective about how they teach and how future teachers are prepared. We conclude with some recommendations for teacher educators and teachers who are interested in engaging with the questions we raise.

Amos: As the instructor of the cross-department seminar, I sat with a different group each session. On the evening that Kelly presented her book review, I was sitting with a group of doctoral students from special education and education for the deaf and hard of hearing. An underlying thesis of Kirkland's book is that young Black men value literacy and use literacy in their lives, but in ways that are invisible, ignored, or silenced in school. Noting that the author did not give specific strategies for uncovering or developing these nascent literacies, Kelly asked, "What are some ways we can tap into these kinds of literacy experiences in the classroom?" She tagged that prompt with what struck me as a much more interesting question: "Should we?"

In our small group, I tried to get the other participants to see how we as teachers never seem to ask the "should we" question when we are thinking about ways to bring students' home or community cultures into the classroom. I told them about approaches we teach preservice teachers in the Urban-Multicultural Teacher Education program, including strategies encouraged by Lisa Delpit (2006) and others (e.g., Perez, 2000) for using Black English as a starting place for teaching African American students, what Delpit calls "paycheck English." I talked about the discomfort I was feeling as I considered Kelly's "should we" question.

In the small group, and later when the discussion was opened to the whole seminar, I tried to articulate how we as teachers are so focused on our goals of teaching standard forms of academic performance and raising scores on standardized tests that we almost never consider the possibility that we may be appropriating students' cultures for our own purposes. As a group, the doctoral students seemed to see no conflict, saying, "That's what we do. Teaching the curriculum any way we can is our job as teachers." I agreed, restating that that's what we were teaching the preservice teachers. However, I still noted my discomfort, referring back to the primary example in the book Kelly had reviewed.

In *A Search Past Silence*, Kirkland's prime example is a student named Derrick, who kept a personal "book," which he titled *SILENCE*. In it, Derrick included freestyle raps, symbology, research, and art. It read much like a multi-genre autobiography. The teacher who discovered *SILENCE* (and most of the teachers reading the book, I argued) saw the discovery of Derrick's personal journal as an opportunity to *use* that discovery as a tool for teaching paycheck-English writing skills. But what about the artistic integrity of the original work? What about the inherent value of the personal, community, and cultural forms expressed in Derrick's book? What are we saying about expressions of Black culture when teachers merely use them to bring the learning of African American students into line with school expectations?

Kelly: By chance, during the summer after the seminar, I moved into the office next to Amos's. We chatted in the hallway a few times about our shared fascination with the issues raised in the seminar discussion and decided to work together to find our own answers to questions like those listed by Amos. I was also enrolled in two summer courses that focused on linguistics in the classroom and on applying the "Youth Lens" to critique literature and teaching practices. With every new reading and discussion, I kept returning to discussions with Amos and the questions they gave birth to.

Once we had a general plan, I began searching the literature for what, exactly, appropriation is. If Amos and I were going to use a word with strong connotations, we had better have a shared understanding as to what we were making claims about. In their introduction to *Borrowed Power: Essays on Cultural Appropriation*, Ziff and Rao (1997) used the definition of the Writers' Union of Canada, which states that cultural appropriation is "the taking—from a culture that is not one's own—of intellectual property, cultural expressions or artifacts, history and of knowledge and profiting at the expense of the people of that culture" (pp. 1, 24). Within this definition, we have a perpetrator and a victim. Overlay this on our discussion about White teachers bringing Black culture into the classroom, and a racial aspect is introduced that sets up the White teacher as the perpetrator and the Black students as victims. If this dynamic is playing out in classrooms, it is a very damaging relationship to establish between teachers and students.

I went back to Kirkland's (2013) book, *A Search Past Silence*, and his (2009) article, "The Skin We Ink: Tattoos, Literacy, and a New English Education," both based on his ethnographic study of four Black teenage males. The Black literacies revealed in the study included rap lyrics, symbolic drawings, graffiti, tattoos, letters, speeches, answers on government documents, journal entries, and posts on social media. In *A Search Past Silence*, Kirkland focused on sharing these multiple literacies with his readers to illustrate that these four disengaged students in class are not nonliterate, but that they "overflow with language, literacies, and dialogic acts that, [he] suspect[s], go places no one goes in school" (Kirkland, 2013, p. 138). And in his article, he posited that we (teachers) should not deny students these alternate literacies but should broaden our definitions of what constitutes a literate being. This could provide a way to challenge the deficit theory so often attached to Black students and help to change the public's perception of these students as problems (Kirkland, 2009). In both his article and book, Kirkland (2009; 2013) strongly advocates that teachers open their classrooms to new forms of literacy and to think beyond the standardized versions of literacy that are so often privileged in classrooms.

However, Kirkland never suggested that teachers are the ones who should introduce their students to or engage their students in creating alternate forms of literacy. That led me to search for studies conducted in classrooms in which a teacher was using Black cultural elements in his or her lesson plans and the effect that had on the students. A recent study by Kim and Pulido (2015) did just that. Kim shadowed Florence, a Black teacher in Chicago who self-reported as using hip-hop to engage her all-Black class in her lessons. She chose several songs and used them to engage students in vocabulary activities and writing exercises. However, when Kim interviewed students regarding their thoughts about Florence using hip-hop in the classroom, they balked. In fact, one student asked, *"She do, what?"* (Kim & Pulido, 2015, p. 23). Most of Florence's students did not even realize she was using hip-hop to engage them; instead, they completely dismissed her efforts by claiming she was too "old-school" and accused her of trying too hard "to study up" on it and of choosing songs the students didn't even like (pp. 23–24). Even though Florence's students respected her and worked hard for her, Kim and Pulido claimed that integrating rap into her lessons was *not* a contributing factor in her establishing a culturally relevant pedagogy as described by Ladson-Billings (1995).

Petchauer (2009) explained that the popularity of using hip-hop (and, we would argue, other alternative forms of Black cultural expression) in classroom curricula has been rising because of scholars such as Ladson-Billings, Gay, Giroux, and Friere, who argue that classrooms need to be more culturally inclusive and reflective of the students who inhabit them. However, Petchauer found that there is little research that helps us understand whether integrating hip-hop into lessons "help[s] students learn course material, improve[s] their motivation to learn, or increase[s] graduation rates" (p. 964). Even though many teachers are "drawing non-traditional spaces such as hip-hop into traditional schooling spaces . . . hop[ing] to increase their students' engagement, foster a cultural climate based on community, develop critical literacy, empower identities, and create more opportunities for student voice both inside and outside of the classroom" (Kim & Pulido, 2015, pp. 19–20), scholars such as Petchauer, Kim, Pulido, and even Ladson-Billings herself believe that many teachers who are engaging in using hip-hop in the classroom are misinterpreting and even corrupting the underlying tenets of what culturally relevant pedagogy (CRP) really is. This is partially because teachers often select socially conscious songs that usually do not align with students' tastes for more commercial hip-hop (Petchauer, 2009) and also because teachers are assuming that because students are Black or are young, they will identify with hip-hop. These flaws represent two strikes against establishing a genuine CRP.

Returning to the idea of appropriation, in her article "Using Hip Hop in Schools: Are We Appreciating Culture or Raping Rap?" Brown (2005) feared that most teachers use hip-hop in the classroom to "get 'those' students to write, analyze, and critique the literature we *really* want them to appreciate" (para. 1). Rather than honoring rap as an art form in and of itself and educating students about its history, underpinnings, and purpose, teachers are merely attempting to engage students for their own educational ends. Ironically, much of rap is vehemently anti-establishment, but what we are seeing is the art form being inserted into one of the most well-established American institutions—the classroom.

DIALOGUE

The next section of this chapter will take the form of a dialogue between the authors. It is an edited elaboration of conversations the authors had concerning issues we see as central to figuring out the place of Black-student culture in the school curriculum. Interchanges are organized around a set of questions that evolved across a series of tape-recorded meetings.

1. What do we mean by *appropriation*?

Amos: In the opening comments, we've got this technical definition of appropriation from the Writers' Union of Canada that's about profiting from taking intellectual property from a cultural group that is not your own. So, when I read back over that, it's a writer's group that wrote that, so I'm thinking it has to do with indigenous people of Canada who have been ripped off by writers who have taken their material and published it or sold it and made a profit at the expense of the original writers and creators. So that's connected to our discussion because it's about culture. But, it's hard to argue that teachers are profiting monetarily from using Black cultural expressions or artifacts when they teach. I just looked at a more ordinary definition of appropriation and found: the act of taking something for one's own use, typically without the owner's permission.

Kelly: Sounds to me like we are talking about something in between. I think the cultural dimension of the Canadian writers' definition is important to our discussions. Teachers may not be profiting financially, but they are using Black cultural forms for their own ends, and they are not asking permission.

Amos: Yes, so our notion of appropriation, as you've just described it, would be an apt description of what often happens when White teachers use Black cultural expressions, like hip-hop or call-and-response sermons, to teach standard English?

Kelly: Right. There may not be financial winners and losers, but there is still the element of the dominant cultural group appropriating subordinates' "property" for its own purposes.

Amos: So, maybe the rightness or wrongness of those purposes is an important element in the debate.

2. What do we mean by culturally relevant education?

Kelly: Seems like if we are going to use the term, we need to be clear about what we mean by culturally relevant education and how that term relates to culturally relevant teaching and culturally relevant pedagogy.

Amos: Yeah, so looks like we will rely on Aronson and Laughter's (2016) new article in the *Review of Educational Research* to talk about culturally relevant education. A simple view is that Aronson and Laughter just took Gay's (2010) culturally relevant teaching (CRT) and merged it with Ladson-Billings's (1995) notion of culturally relevant pedagogy (CRP) to make culturally relevant education (CRE). Of course, it's more complicated than that.

Kelly: I think CRP is making your students very aware that your classroom is a site for social change. Ladson-Billings (1995) called it a "pedagogy of opposition" (p. 160). As a teacher, you acknowledge the power structure of standardized language and tests, and you are going to teach them how to negotiate that so they can be successful in that system. But then you're also opening up your classroom to studying real-world problems and validating different cultures, and acknowledging that the White culture has been dominant in schools. Both CRP and CRT are based on similar theoretical and political frameworks, but I think CRT is more about *how* teachers apply these frameworks in the classroom. Gay (2010) talked about making students' learning experiences more relevant by connecting classroom lessons to the "cultural knowledge, prior experiences, frames of reference, and performance styles of ethnically diverse students" (p. 31). And I think that when teachers try to apply CRT principles, that's when we run the risk of appropriating. Because we're in a hurry and we're putting lessons together fast, and we're thinking, "Well, let me pull this rap lyric, let me pull this graffiti art in order to engage the kids." But, I don't think merely including these elements in lesson plans is what Gay meant by CRT or Ladson-Billings meant by CRP.

Amos: Sounds like you are saying that teachers who are responsible for teaching a lot of content every day may be trying to "do" CRT or CRP but are only working on the surface of these conceptual frameworks. So, what really counts is what teachers *think* those concepts mean—not what they actually mean. When teachers bring in bits of Black-student culture, they do it because that's what they think they should be doing. So they might be bringing in hip-hop music or, like in the book your reviewed, trying to use the literacies evident in the kid's journal to teach standard writing. Teachers think they are doing culturally relevant stuff, no matter what you call it, while in reality they may be missing core elements that define cultural relevance and, in effect, appropriating Black-student culture.

Kelly: Aronson and Laughter (2016) said that if you mesh CRT and CRP, you have a focus on social-justice education and the classroom as a site for social change—what they call culturally relevant education. I think Aronson and Laughter want to be sure that CRE is not used as a checklist. It's not "if you do this, this, and this, then you're using CRE." It's more of a posture as a teacher that you appreciate and value all students' cultures and that they are welcome and involved in the classroom. So, just bringing hip-hop lyrics in to engage students, no, I don't think is a form of CRE.

Amos: But the Aronson and Laughter piece is a review of the literature, and they cited several studies as examples of CRE that looked to me as though teachers might be appropriating Black-student cultural artifacts for their own purposes.

Kelly: Maybe. They highlight a study, in which Morrell and Duncan-Andrade (2002) included hip-hop pedagogy in language arts instruction, that concluded: "Hip-hop pedagogy was one example of how we might close cultural gaps and see the power and potential of pedagogy grounded in CRE" (Aronson & Laughter, 2016, p. 27). I wrote, "Do we agree with that?" in the margin next to that quote. Aronson and Laughter go on to say that the hip-hop pedagogy in this study was an attempt to "forge a critical discourse in students' lives" and "engage in a critical dialogue and make connections to larger social and political issues" (p. 27). So that sounds more like CRE than appropriation.

Amos: Yeah, that's a good point, but I'm not sure it's a complete answer. I hate circular arguments; but, if we use the phrase "culturally relevant education" the way Aronson and Laughter describe it, we may end up saying that if you *really* do CRE, then the chances of appropriating student culture go down. My issue still is teachers doing their best to implement their understanding of CRE but leaving out the critical analysis parts so that what they do actually works against CRE objectives.

3. Is it appropriation to use Black cultural forms (like hip-hop) to teach academics?

Amos: So, is it really appropriation by our hybrid definition? We don't know yet, do we?

Kelly: No, I don't think we do. I mean, do you? Even though there's no financial gain involved, it looks as though White teachers are taking artifacts from Black culture and using them for their own ends, and without permission. What do you think?

Amos: So for sure it's for our own use, but you could argue it also benefits the kids. That gets us into a philosophical discussion about why they are in school, what we should be teaching and how, and how it really benefit kids. So it's not perfectly clear.

Kelly: I don't think so either. I don't think it's perfectly clear. Because teachers are there to do a job, and their kids do have to learn, and if one way to do it is to reel kids into the culture of the classroom through pop culture, Black-student culture, then that's a means to an end.

Amos: The other part of it is "without their permission." So maybe that is a hook we could use. If we are taking Black-student culture and using it to accomplish our own ends, and students didn't give permission or they resent that in some way, they perceive that as appropriation, and then that feels wrong. But, maybe if we have their permission, it would not feel so much like manipulation. You said last time that if we got them to bring it in themselves, somehow it would make it more legit. But maybe that just takes the con game to another level—you pick the material, then I'll use it for my own ends.

Kelly: Yeah, in the Kim and Pulido (2015) study in my review, the African American teacher used hip-hop, and her students pushed back against that—not her—but against that form of teaching. They felt like she was trying too hard; she was trying to be too cool. So I think it does have to be a negotiation with the students. I think it has to be a conversation, not something you are trying to do on the sly. And, in the Aronson and Laughter (2016) article, they wrote a lot about motivating students to appreciate their own cultures and not feeling like they have to leave it at the classroom door because it's not welcome in the room. So I do think it matters who's bringing in the Black-student culture. Are the kids bringing it in, and then you're taking it up and using it in the learning? Or are you bringing it in and saying, "I think this is what you are going to like, this is how I'm going to hook you." And it might not be authentic on the teacher's part.

Amos: Right, so maybe what the kids think is going on is what really counts. It doesn't really matter if the teacher believes that he or she is not appropriating, but if the kids feel like they are being patronized or conned or used, that's what matters. Maybe it's not appropriation if the kids are fully aware of what's going on, it's not some kind of subversive strategy. If we also talk about it like the author of the book you reviewed (Kirkland, 2013) as letting kids see that there are many literacies at work here, and each one ought to be valued. That feels way different from: "Okay, you've got your rap lyric here. Let's translate that, let's take that and fix it"—like it is some-how inferior poetry. Acknowledge it as a genre in its own right. And maybe that gets around the complaint of the students that the Chicago teacher was bringing in homogenized stuff that she thought the kids should be thinking, rather than what they're really into. That makes me think though that some of the stuff they're really into would be sort of tough to put up on the board.

Kelly: I definitely agree. I know, because if we have students bringing in the songs that they like or cultural artifacts that they like, then most teachers feel like they have to say, "Make sure it's school appropriate," and there goes the cycle again. We say we value Black-student culture, but only the white-washed version that's appropriate for school.

Amos: Yeah, this is tough territory to negotiate.

4. What's wrong with using Black English to teach "standard English"?

Amos: All right, so I brought this up during the doctoral seminar that started this conversation. I told the doctoral students about how my reading of Lisa Delpit has influenced what we do in our Urban-Multicultural Teacher Education program. In fact, we are reading Delpit's (2013) newer book, *Multiplication Is for White People*, with our preservice teachers this term. In the original book, *Other People's Children* (Delpit, 2006), she gave a powerful example of taking speeches from Black ministers and then having the kids translate those as a way to teach kids what she calls "paycheck English." So I thought that was a great approach until we started asking these questions, and now I'm wondering what's wrong with that.

Kelly: I think a lot of times what teachers intend and what students perceive or what they experience don't always align. So I guess my critique would be that if teachers are having students translate or correct the speech, they're sending the message to students, whether they mean to or not, that African American Vernacular English is incorrect, that there's something wrong with it. But, I think that as a teacher, you have to frontload that with the idea that we all speak in different ways. I'm White; I speak differently with my family, with my sons, with my friends, and in my classroom. We *all* speak in different ways, but there is a more widely accepted way that gives you a chance to participate in what Delpit (2006) calls the "culture of power," so let's make sure that we give kids a chance to learn that as well. I think that's the part that teachers leave out sometimes; and instead, they just present these activities of let's fix this or let's interpret this and make it "right."

Amos: Yeah, I agree again that what matters is what the kids think is happening. In her book *Multiplication Is for White People*, Delpit (2013) described how a teacher in Florida teaches her students to assess their own and their peers' writing by adopting the perspective of "the little white ladies in Tallahassee!" (p. 141). I'm just not sure that when we say "a more accepted way" or reference "little White ladies" who will be grading their work, students don't internalize the subtext that their own language is "unacceptable" and needs translating—especially if it's a White teacher saying it.

Kelly: But what kids think is going on is bigger than just an isolated phrase or two. If teachers have built a classroom that could be characterized as implementing culturally relevant education, then activities like translating Black English into paycheck English would not have to be negative experiences. In the Delpit and Dowdy (2008) book *The Skin That We Speak,* there's a chapter by Delpit, "No Kinda Sense," in which she writes of going into a school because of the achievement gap. She started coming up with possible projects for different subject areas to incorporate Black students' interests and cultural heritage in their classes, but it was much deeper than superficial surface stuff. If the girls were very interested in hair, because that's an important part of their cultural experience, there was a project involving English class by researching the history of braiding in Africa, involving the chemistry class in the solutions that were used on hair, involving the geometry class in examining braiding patterns, or tessellations. She found that because the students were personally invested in the topic, they were more apt to use formal English in their reports and presentations. So I think imbedding standard academic forms inside a classroom where it's clear that the teacher respects and values the children's culture is different from just teaching kids to perform in a way that will satisfy those who have power over them.

5. What are we saying about Black cultural forms when we use them only to teach "standard" forms?

Kelly: So we talked about this last time, and I think we said that if Black culture is just used as a way to accomplish the teacher's academic aims, then teachers really are signaling that they believe that the Black forms are inferior, that they're deficient in some way. But if we take an approach imbedded in culturally relevant education, it wouldn't be about just teaching them the "right way" to do it.

Amos: But, Delpit (2006) talks about giving African American students the tools they need to participate in the culture of power. Some scholars and activists disagree, arguing that we are selling out Black kids by telling them they need to conform in order to make it in mainstream society. But Delpit is consistent across all of her writing in saying that Black kids still need to learn the language and also acknowledge the values that are expressed through people's actions in order to succeed. Otherwise, it's unfair if you don't explicitly teach those to kids, she says. They don't have a chance of succeeding in mainstream society.

Kelly: I definitely agree with that, and I read a book about "code-meshing" (Young et al., 2014), and it kind of slammed code switching. I think the authors shouldn't have been so critical of code switching because, if Delpit is right, we do have to give all students tools to succeed in the dominant culture. But the authors took it a step further and said that it's important again to have those conversations with your students. This is the dominant language, and this is what employers are looking for, and I'm going to give you the tools, and now you have a choice. You have a choice to do that—to use paycheck English and play the game, or you have a choice to not—to push back against that—but there are consequences. There are consequences to that choice. So, I don't know. I keep going back to explaining to the students . . . and I don't know why I'm assuming teachers don't do that. But I feel like a lot of times teachers don't make their pedagogy transparent to their students. I think you have to tell students *why* you are doing something and hope they're going to internalize those purposes.

Amos: I think maybe part of the reason why that doesn't happen is that teachers are afraid—not of their students' reaction to exposing their pedagogical logic, but of parents and school administrators. Like our urban-multicultural students are really afraid that they are going to get blowback for using the culturally relevant and critical pedagogical approaches we teach. When they do try these approaches, they are a little more covert about what they are doing. So I don't think they feel comfortable sharing that with the students or anyone else; but maybe that's part of the reason why it's not working—or that it's not happening very much after they leave us.

Kelly: In one of the articles I read (Baker, 2008) a teacher, during her first days of class, divides her students into similar home-language groups. So, if you have a group of students meshing Spanish and English, or a group of students speaking African American Vernacular English, or a group of student who speak "proper" English, you put them together. Within their groups, they do a profile of what their language is like, and they talk about, for the first few days, how everyone's language is different but how they all have sound grammatical structures and patterns and deep meanings. So they start out by appreciating their home languages and then move toward mastering paycheck English. And I thought that was a powerful way. Again, rather than the teacher standing up there saying, "I know we don't all talk like this, but we have to learn standard English," she helped lead them to discover that kind of dynamic on their own through examining their home languages.

Amos: So it seems like we are developing a theme around the idea that it's possible to bring Black student culture into the classroom in ways that can lead to progress in school learning but that it's very difficult at the least.

6. Can White teachers really connect with Black student culture? Can they really implement culturally relevant education practices?

Kelly: What are your initial thoughts on that?

Amos: I think they can try to approach connecting with their students' cultural backgrounds and experiences. It's always going to be a journey, and all you can do is try to move forward in improving understanding and making connections—at least that's what we tell our students and ourselves. Kids can tell when you are really trying to connect, and they can tell if you are posing, if you're just pretending. They can see right through that. We're discouraged because of all the stuff we are seeing in schools and in society. I guess I continue to think it's possible to implement CRE, but based on my experience as a White professor working with White preservice teachers, it's going to be tough.

Kelly: And I think it depends on the individual students and their families' stances on race relations. I think that some White teachers can really connect using Black student culture. And I think some can't. And I think some kids will let them connect, and I think some kids won't let them connect. I don't know that we can lump that all into one answer. I can't imagine saying yes, but I can't imagine saying no, either. Because if we say no, then we might as well just quit.

Amos: For sure! We've been busting our butts, some of us for a long time, to try to get CRE going. I don't want to give up. Still, I wonder sometimes if all the effort and angst are making any real difference. I did a little study with students in our program a few years ago and tied one of the key outcomes to the old Pink Floyd *Brick in the Wall* song (Hatch, 2008). It's a bit cynical, but it's possible that we are all just bricks in the wall. Maybe the hard work is more about us than kids, families, and communities that are different from us.

Kelly: I need to read your study, but I still think we have to keep trying. Even though we can never be perfect, we have to be the best teachers we can be, and I think that means trying to connect with our students and teach in ways that improve their life chances. The Aronson and Laughter (2016) article reviewed studies that show that CRE can be effective, that it can actually do some good academically and help strengthen affective areas like motivation, confidence, and students' interest in the content. The White teachers and future teachers I work with want to make a difference, and if CRE provides a conceptual framework that helps them make a difference, we can't give up.

7. How can White teachers reach Black students if they don't connect with the students' lives?

Amos: I mean connecting with students' lives is the premise for all good teaching, and it's critical to CRE and other culturally relevant approaches. Delpit (2013) says it baldly: "If the curriculum we use to teach our children does not connect in positive ways to the culture young people bring to school, it is doomed to failure" (p. 21). We don't want to come away saying it's impossible for White teachers to connect to Black student culture, but it sort of creates this conundrum. What do we do if we don't do this? If we need to get to this place, how can we do it without appropriating Black student culture?

Kelly: So, a premise of CRE is that there have to be connections among school and home, community, family. We both work with White teachers, or preservice teachers, and they get the gist of this. I mean they understand the importance of making these connections, but doing it is really tough. They're afraid that they can't reach Black kids.

Amos: Yes, they understand, and I think they want to try to connect, but I agree that they are unsure and afraid.

Kelly: This reminds me of conversations I've had with professors and graduate students about teachers not knowing how to talk about race. I feel like it's the elephant in the room—I'm a White teacher, and I am trying to reach a Black student through making connections. I think part of doing CRE is having conversations with students about the power structure and about race and about how it plays out in the classroom. And making sure that your African American students have a voice. That they're allowed to say "I see what you're doing here. You're not really appreciating my culture. I feel like you're bringing it in to try to get me interested in the lesson." And that's an OK statement to make in a classroom. I feel like that goes back to some of our preservice teachers and their reservations about how they can reach students. It's especially hard to talk about race because racial tensions are so high right now, and it's just a very hard topic to talk about in the classroom for so many teachers.

Amos: I'm with you. It is super hard to talk about race on campus right now and maybe more difficult in school classrooms. But, maybe getting over that obstacle would be a big step toward helping teachers get past using Black student culture to accomplish their own ends and begin seeing and addressing the structural elements and unequal power relations that characterize society and schooling.

8. Is it right? Should we use Black student culture to teach school curriculum?

Amos: Yeah, I'm ambivalent about it for sure. Is it appropriation to use Black cultural forms like hip-hop to teach academics? It sounds like where we are is that if it is done out in the open and the kids participate and OK it, or they bring the stuff in themselves, then it's not really appropriation. The tricky part is also getting them to buy into the idea that they need the academic curriculum—that they need to do well on the standardized test. There's conflict there. Because if you're teaching kids that their language is legit, that it has a sound structure, it's just as complex and meaningful as any other language form, then comes the big *but*: you still have to use the standard forms in order to make it in school and society.

Kelly: So you're saying you don't think you can do both? You don't think you can practice culturally relevant education and teach Black students to value paycheck English or motivate them to do well on standardized tests?

Amos: Well, I don't know at this point if you can or cannot, but I know that there is a real tension there. I like the idea that if students are fully aware of what's going on and they really are engaged and motivated by it, that's OK. I just think very few teachers, White or Black, are at that place.

Kelly: And I am not saying that I was there, but I taught ACT prep for a few years—it was a required class for juniors. And I had a hard time with that. I had a hard time with my whole day revolving around a standardized test. But we talked a lot about standardized tests, why they're fair, why they're unfair, and we staged it around: I'm here to help you beat the system. But I don't know how well that worked.

Amos: Well, you know what you said earlier about the teacher who explained how the system works, then told the students it was up to them to take it or leave it. Here are your options: It's on you. No matter how much we care or how well we think we lay things out, some students are going to be conscientious objectors and say this is bullshit.

Kelly: For sure, but I still think that as a teacher, if you are going to bring hip-hop or graffiti art or symbology through tattoos into the classroom, I think that you have to have that conversation about appreciating cultures and multiple literacies. You have to acknowledge that hip-hop was born in pushing back against the establishment, and other Black cultural elements are pushing back against the dominant culture. I think you have to have that conversation with your students. I don't think you can just come in with a cultural piece to try to reel them in. But I think you need to set it up as "This is why I brought it in, you are welcome to bring more examples that you see in your lives." But I really think for you to do culturally relevant education, you have to make that process clear to the students. You have to make it clear that your classroom is a site for social justice or a classroom for social change. And not, I'm just trying to trick you into . . .

Amos: . . . how to pass the test. Which is something that Ladson-Billings (2006) talks about. It's not about passing the test. It's about helping kids be learners for life and changing their perspectives on their own culture and majority culture.

Kelly: And I think the best teachers can do both. I think the best teachers can create learners for life but also make them successful on standardized tests. Because it's hard to throw that by the wayside. Testing more or less defines success for students and teachers in schools today.

Amos: So, is it appropriation? One answer is: "Well, what if it is appropriation? What else can we do?"

Kelly: So, if it's appropriation, and we're saying we shouldn't use Black student culture to try to engage Black kids in the classroom, then what else do we do?

Amos: Right. So it's possible, I guess, as it has been for generations, to just be the White teacher who lives inside the culture of power, has the cultural capital and the cultural knowledge, and just teaches the standard curriculum whether the kids get it or not. That model's not working too well.

Kelly: No. We both know we don't agree with that. For me, it goes back to exploring why so many Black students don't feel like school is structured for them or set up for them or welcoming for them. We kind of know the answer to that.

Amos: Yeah.

Kelly: But then, I definitely think we have to bring their culture in and appreciate their culture for real, and not appropriate it for lessons. I think it's *how* you do it—the way you do it—that counts. Like you said, kids can see right through teachers who are trying to manipulate them.

Amos: Oh, yeah, if you are faking it or playing them, they'll know that immediately. They'll play you back. So then the big question I think we've been trying to answer since we started doing this is "Is it right?" I guess I'm at a place, like I said a few minutes ago, that it's right as long as it's open. Out on the table. The students have to buy into it, or at least have the chance to buy into it. Maybe there is a step in there where they give permission, to go back to our hybrid definition. It doesn't have to be an active permission, but it could be. The way schools are set up right now, is there a way around teaching the standard forms that appear on tests?

Kelly: No, there is no way around it. But there is a way around it being a dominant, oppressive force in the classroom, where students know if you don't speak correctly or you don't write correctly, your ideas aren't valued. Which reminds me of the old-school English teacher who doesn't really care what you're saying, but only your grammar and spelling matter. I think CRT, or CRP, or CRE, whatever we call it, are legitimate frameworks for providing educational experiences for all children. We should be doing that, but I think we have to understand the complexity and nuances of these approaches, not turn them into a checklist, or pull a cool hip-hop activity out of the blue to teach a new concept, which then I think turns it into appropriation.

Amos: I love that. I mean, I think it captures where we are at the moment, at least our shared sentiment.

Kelly: But are we saying anything that is provocative? If we said that, would people not say, "Yeah, I agree with that."

Amos: I think laying out the struggle and sharing a little of how we got to this point is what's useful to others because, to me, it's the friction between these forces that matters. If people don't struggle with that, then they're not going to get to a meaningful resolution—no matter what that might be. So, I think when it's framed as a journey and we take people on our journey, then I think it's something new to some folks and would stir questions that some folks have never asked. Just to say that you may do hip-hop in your classroom and not be doing CRE will be provocative for some.

Kelly: Going back to the Kirkland (2013) book I reviewed, when the teacher found the student's book, his journal, she was amazed at it. And when she told him that, he said, "There's nothing you can do to help me."

Amos: Yeah, you mean well, but give me back my book.

Kelly: And I wonder if that is an illustration of that student's frustration with school in general or his statement about having his culture appropriated for the purposes of the teacher. At some level, it's like we need to restructure our whole school system to make sure all cultures know that their literacies and beliefs are welcomed and valued. For me, that's another tension I struggle with. How much can I do working within a system that systematically disadvantages so many young people? How many other children face their teachers every day, believing "You can't help me"?

Amos: Way too many! I have the same frustrations, but, like you have said throughout our talks, we cannot give up. We cannot give up trying to make sure we always honor everyone's cultural backgrounds and experiences, never appropriate students' cultural expressions for our own purposes or without their knowledge and permission, and always do our best to apply the principles of culturally relevant education as comprehensively as we can. We must remember that applying CRE in the classroom includes helping students to critique a system that oppresses them in many ways, giving them tools for resisting that oppression may be a way to change their lives and challenge the system.

REFLECTIONS AND RECOMMENDATIONS

Amos: Making recommendations is tricky territory. One of the big lessons for us seems to be that the process of seriously studying questions like the ones we asked is what counts as much as any conclusions we might draw. So I would recommend that university instructors engage prospective teacher educators (i.e., advanced graduate students) and future teachers (i.e., undergrad and master's students working toward licensure) in conversations like ours. Doctoral seminars like the one in which this topic came to light for us could provide a good venue for getting these issues on the table. Future teacher educators could read materials like those in our references and bring their own readings, experiences, and perspectives to classroom discussions. For me, these sessions need to be dialogues, not lectures.

It gets really tricky to think about introducing the notion of appropriation of Black student culture to future teachers at the same time we are trying to get them to understand and apply principles of culturally relevant education. In our Urban-Multicultural Teacher Education program, we made culturally relevant pedagogy a centerpiece of our efforts. However, even as you and I were having our recorded talks in preparation of this article, I did not directly address my concerns with my teacher-education instructional team or with the preservice teachers in our classes. I did not want to sidetrack the efforts of my colleagues or cloud the understanding of my students. Having completed this process, I think I would be braver now.

Again, for me, just getting future educators to acknowledge the possibility that they may do a disservice to their students by treating Black student culture merely as a means to an academic end is a pretty big step. Gaining an understanding of culturally relevant education that goes beyond using hip-hop-sounding rhymes to teach basic skills or studying classic rap lyrics alongside traditional poetry will not happen if future teachers are *told* they need a more nuanced perspective. Like their more seasoned counterparts, they also need opportunities to explore, discuss, and come to their own conclusions.

For many (mature and novice) educators, just the idea of implementing principles of CRE in schools that are obsessed with accountability as measured on standards-based assessments is daunting. They are sure that by using CRE they are going to upset parents and administrators or, worse, find themselves featured in right-wing media and trolled on the internet. Thinking about ways to introduce students to practices that run counter to the mainstream made me think of a chapter in which Susan Groenke and I (Hatch & Groenke, 2009) reported findings from a study we did of professors' approaches to introducing critical pedagogical approaches to education students. The three recommendations below are synthesized from several of those teacher educators' suggestions. I think they make sense for guiding the exploration of the sensitive issues raised in this chapter:

1. Provide salient, concrete examples that demonstrate that a complex view of using Black student culture in the classroom is possible and necessary.
2. Build relationships with students and avoid confrontations that make students feel cornered when they are uncomfortable with challenging issues.
3. Encourage the development of critical thinking in students and give them opportunities to identify their own issues related to CSE and potential appropriation.

Kelly: During the presentation that got this reflective process started, I did not know that asking a follow-up question of "should we?" would prompt our continued conversation, but I am glad it did. Upon returning to the high-school classroom as a ninth- and twelfth-grade ELA teacher, I find myself asking this a lot. My school has the capacity and the desire to facilitate paperless classrooms—but should we? My ELA department has created uni-form teaching units complete with preselected themes, texts from which to choose, and a common assessment—but should we? As the winds of educa-tion around me change, I have adopted the stance of "I know we *can* do that, but the better question is '*should* we?'" Sometimes, I feel as though I am just resistant to change, but other times I remind myself that the difference be-tween teaching methods and pedagogy and asking "should we?" is pedagogy at work.

In my ninth-grade ELA class, the anchor texts I can choose to teach consist mostly of those by White male authors (e.g., Frost, Shakespeare, Wiesel), which runs counter to the aims of culturally relevant education (Aronson & Laughter, 2016). This has reminded me that including Black (along with other diverse peoples') culture, authors, and subject matter needs to be the norm. It needs to be woven into the fabric and philosophy of the curriculum. Not as a novelty. Not as a bridge. And, definitely not as an example of something that needs to be corrected.

As teachers, if we are seeking to authentically include, honor, and pro-mote our students' cultures in our classrooms, then we are making strides to provide and practice CRE. But if we are pulling in cultural artifacts that we think will hook them into what we really want them to focus on—usually a White normative learning task—then I believe we are engaging in cultural appropriation. One small way I have worked to push back against the White-normed curriculum that has been imposed upon my students and me is to engage in daily independent reading (Kittle, 2013). We read books of our choosing for the first fifteen minutes of class, and I have made sure to include diverse authors in my classroom library (e.g., #blacklivesmatter is a book category on one of my shelves). I also model reading books written by non-White and female authors and share what is happening in the book with my students.

Should I do this? Yes. I am not reading or promoting these books as a way to engage students with reading, and then with a sleight of hand, taking their books and replacing them with normative texts. I am reading and pro-moting these books because they counteract the damage that can occur to diverse students' psyches when they don't see their faces reflected in the curriculum and to all students when they think only White male voices matter. My basic recommendation for classroom teachers is that as we create learning environments, plan lessons, and choose activities, I hope we will pause and contemplate the question "should I?" If we are to practice culturally relevant pedagogy, we have to remember that it is just that—a pedagogy. It is a philosophy, a belief, a sociopolitical stance; it is not a bag of tricks.

REFERENCES

Aronson, B., & Laughter, J. (2016). The theory and practice of culturally relevant education: A synthesis of research across content areas. *Review of Educational Research, 86*(1), 163–206.

Baker, J. (2008). Trilingualism. In L. Delpit & J. K. Dowdy (Eds.), *The skin that we speak: Thoughts on language and culture in the classroom* (pp. 51–61). New York, NY: The New Press.

Brown, A. (2005). Using Hip Hop in schools: Are we appreciating culture or raping rap? *The Council Chronicle.* Retrieved from http://www.ncte.org/pubs/chron/formembers/123024.html.

Delpit, L. (2006). *Other people's children: Cultural conflict in the classroom.* New York, NY: The New Press.

Delpit, L. (2008). No kinda sense. In L. Delpit & J. K. Dowdy (Eds.), *The skin that we speak: Thoughts on language and culture in the classroom* (pp. 31–48). New York, NY: The New Press.

Delpit, L. (2013). *"Multiplication is for white people": Raising expectations for other people's children.* New York: The New Press.

Delpit, L. & Dowdy, J. K. (Eds.), *The skin that we speak: Thoughts on language and culture in the classroom.* New York, NY: The New Press.

Gay, G. (2010). *Culturally responsive teaching: Theory, research, and practice* (2nd ed.). New York, NY: Teachers College Press.

Hatch, J. A. (2008). Preservice teachers' perspectives on critical pedagogy for urban teaching: Yet another brick in the wall? *Teacher Education and Practice, 21,* 128–45.

Hatch, J. A., & Groenke, S. L. (2009). Issues in critical teacher education: Insights from the field. In S. L. Groenke and J. A. Hatch (Eds.), *Critical pedagogy and teacher education in the neoliberal era: Small openings* (pp. 63–83). New York, NY: Springer.

Kim, J., & Pulido, I. (2015). Examining hip-hop as culturally relevant pedagogy. *Journal of Curriculum and Pedagogy, 12*(1), 17–35.

Kirkland, D. E. (2009). The skin we ink: Tattoos, literacy, and a new English education. *English Education, 41*(4), 375–95.

Kirkland, D. E. (2013). *A search past silence: The literacy of young Black men.* New York, NY: Teachers College Press.

Kittle, P. (2013). *Book love: Developing depth, stamina, and passion in adolescent readers.* Portsmouth, NH: Heinemann.

Ladson-Billings, G. (1995). Toward a theory of culturally relevant pedagogy. *American Educational Research Journal, 32,* 465–91.

Morrell, E., & Duncan-Andrade, J. M. R. (2002). Promoting academic literacy with urban youth through engaging hip-hop culture. *English Journal, 91*(6), 88–92.

Perez, S. A. (2000). Using Ebonics or Black English as a bridge to teaching standard English. *Contemporary Education, 71*(4), 34.

Petchauer, E. (2009). Framing and reviewing hip-hop educational research. *Review of Educational Research, 79*(2), 946–78.

Wallace, K. (2016). Review of *A Search Past Silence: The Literacy of Young Black Men*, by D. Kirkland. *English Journal, 105*(6), 87.

Young, V. A., Barrett, R., Young-Rivera, Y., & Lovejoy, K. B. (2014). *Other people's English: Code-meshing, code-switching, and African American literacy*. New York, NY: Teachers College Press.

Ziff, B., & Rao, P. V. (1997). Introduction to cultural appropriation: A framework for analysis. In B. Ziff & P. V. Rao (Eds.), *Borrowed power: Essays on cultural appropriation* (pp. 1–27). New Brunswick, NJ: Rutgers University Press.

Chapter Three

Improving Public Education by Creating Sanctuary in Schools

A Response to Stress and Trauma in Children and Adolescents Growing Up in Poverty

Eileen Santiago, JoAnne Ferrara, Sarah M. Yanosy, and Kerron Norman

The landscape of American public schools is changing with increasingly large numbers of students growing up poor (Berliner, 2006) and facing the impact of adverse childhood experiences, trauma, and chronic stress (Bloom, 2011). This confluence of factors requires that educators take a more holistic approach to educating their students than the singularly narrow focus on standardized achievement-test performance that currently exists. Such a holistic approach, referred to in this chapter as "whole child education," helps to ensure success both in the immediate and long-term trajectory of students' lives.

Promising developments have recently emerged that synthesize knowledge and research from the fields of social work, psychology, neuroscience, and education. This emerging trend has also served to deeply enhance our understanding of what constitutes "best practice" in schools and validates what educators have always known: that to improve students' academic success, we must begin to address those factors, often occurring beyond the classroom, that serve as obstacles to strong social-emotional and cognitive development.

ANDRUS, a leading provider and pioneer of services for families and children in the field of trauma-informed care, has spearheaded a number of trailblazing efforts to take a clinical model for care, employed in residential and mental health settings, into the public school arena. In doing so, AN-DRUS established a public/private partnership with two public school districts located outside of New York City, each with high levels of poverty and situated in communities found to have significant levels of trauma. This trauma has been associated with the high rates of such adverse childhood experiences as juvenile detention admissions, substance abuse within the home, and reports of neglect or abuse.

ANDRUS began its efforts to transform schools through the dissemination of the Sanctuary Model, a trauma-sensitive model for treatment and organizational change that enables the school community to be better able to respond to the needs of all of its members, with a special focus on children and families experiencing chronic stress, trauma, and adversity. A critical element of the Creating Sanctuary in Schools Project, described in this chapter, recognizes that teachers and administrators working in high-stress communities have often experienced trauma themselves.

The Sanctuary Model actively seeks to respond to the enormous need for greater professional awareness and expertise so that educational practitioners can become trauma informed and better able to respond to the challenges of life in classrooms. Moreover, this initiative seeks to increase the resilience of all members of the school community through capacity building. ANDRUS's Sanctuary Institute faculty and educational practitioners thus joined forces to implement a "tool kit" of strategies for promoting self-reflection and personal safety; establishing developmentally appropriate learning environments that help ease stress and trauma; and establishing positive relational engagement among all members of the school community as a way to improve both student and organizational outcomes.

ANDRUS's work in school districts began around 2010 through the implementation of school-based mental health clinical partnerships and a small grant to provide Sanctuary training at two schools in Westchester County, New York. As a result of this early work, ANDRUS quickly recognized the tremendous need for service components that would support professional development around trauma. Given both the need for professional development and the receptiveness of the school community to this training, AN-DRUS began to actively pursue funding opportunities to bring the Sanctuary Model to public schools in additional school districts.

DEVELOPMENT OF THE CREATING SANCTUARY IN SCHOOLS PROJECT

Another opportunity presented itself in 2013 when the New York State Office for Children and Family Services selected ANDRUS to participate in a public/private partnership grant to provide professional development around trauma-informed school practices for school faculty and staff in a suburban district outside of New York City (referred to in this chapter as District A). The result was the Creating Sanctuary in Schools Project, an initiative uniquely designed as a sustained program of professional development in four of the district's schools, including two elementary (referred to as P.S. 1A and P.S. 2A) and two middle schools (referred to as M.S. 3A and M.S. 4A). The goals of the Creating Sanctuary in Schools Project were as follows:

- the implementation of well-managed and organized classrooms taught by engaged and trauma-informed teachers and school staff
- the engagement of family members as partners in promoting the social-emotional wellness skills learned at school and strengthened at home
- helping schools develop their capacity to form partnerships that are able to provide additional supports for students and families to counter environmental factors that impede student achievement

The aforementioned goals were consistent with a core value held by ANDRUS over the years. ANDRUS has held steadfastly to the belief that coordinating and maximizing public, nonprofit, and private resources to deliver critical services to students and their families will advance student achievement by improving students' readiness to learn, diminishing disruptive classroom behaviors, and enhancing the school's organizational capacity to respond to adversity, stress, and trauma.

In 2014, the New York State Education Department (NYSED) awarded a community school grant to a school district (referred to as District B) in which ANDRUS maintained a long-standing relationship providing school-based mental health services. This grant would facilitate yet another opportunity for ANDRUS to expand its "Creating Sanctuary in Schools" initiative to include a fifth school (referred to as P.S. 5B). As part of this public/private partnership, ANDRUS had the responsibility of providing support and assistance for both community-school and Sanctuary implementation, along with the delivery of school-based mental health services. Due to its grant status and unlike the other four schools participating in the Sanctuary project, P.S. 5B was the only school designated as a community school.

THE SANCTUARY THEORETICAL FRAMEWORK

The Sanctuary Model represents a trauma-informed method for creating or changing classroom and school-wide culture in order to more effectively provide a cohesive trauma-informed context within which education can take place. Sanctuary is a school-wide culture and practice intervention that targets the school community for intervention. This means that activities and outcomes are designed to treat trauma at the individual, classroom, and school-wide levels. The model is composed of four pillars:

Pillar 1: Understanding Adversity. Understanding what happens to individuals when they are hurt—recognizing behaviors as survival skills and making sense of organizational problems from a trauma perspective.

Pillar 2: Seven Commitments. A set of values (nonviolence, emotional intelligence, democracy, social responsibility, open communication, commitment to social learning, growth and change) that describe the way we agree to be in relationships with each other and treat each other in order to mitigate the effects of trauma.

Pillar 3: S.E.L.F. Framework. A problem-solving and solution-seeking framework used to understand problems and solve them without blaming others or ourselves. The four categories that define the most significant impairments that people face when exposed to trauma and how we measure healing: safety, emotions, loss, and future.

Pillar 4: Tool Kit. The daily practices that reinforce the theory, corresponding values, and the language that build community. To facilitate school implementation, a subset of tools was used in order to honor the belief that education rather than treatment is the goal of all classroom intervention.

PROJECT DESCRIPTION

As described earlier, The Creating Sanctuary in Schools Project was initiated in two school districts outside of New York City. Four of the five participating schools in District A may be described as being in "suburban settings with urban characteristics" including significant percentages of minority students and families living at or below federal poverty guidelines. The fifth school, formally joining the project in the fall of 2014, was part of a city school district (District B) in the same county. Once considered immune to the problems typically associated with large cities (i.e., poverty and adversity, residential mobility, and students with limited English proficiency and interrupted schooling), the county in which both districts were located has experienced rapidly changing demographics over the past fifteen years. As a result, suburban schools encountering similar shifts in their student populations are frequently confronted by many of the same barriers to learning as their urban counterparts.

School District A served approximately 8,000 students in grades pre-K through 12 with a student population that was 76 percent Black, 17 percent Hispanic, 5 percent White, and 1 percent Asian, with 77 percent eligible for free or reduced lunch. Moreover, 8 percent of District A students were identified as limited English proficient and 19 percent had been designated for special education services. In comparison, District B remains one of the largest city school districts in New York State, serving a diverse community with approximately 25,000 students in grades pre-K through 12. At the time of this study, the demographics of its student population were: 21 percent Black, 18 percent White, 0 percent American Indian/Alaska Native, 5 percent Asian/Pacific Islander, 1 percent multiracial, and 55 percent Hispanic, with 75 percent of all students eligible for free or reduced lunch. Moreover, 12 percent of District B students had been designated limited English proficient and 16 percent designated for special education services.

Prior to the start of the project, ANDRUS representatives met with the superintendents in both districts to discuss the grant opportunity and potential partnership. After a series of leadership meetings held to identify specific academic and social problems impacting school climate and student performance, district superintendents enthusiastically agreed that a partnership with ANDRUS, focused on trauma-informed practices, would benefit their schools. These district leaders then selected project schools with needs that were commensurate with project goals and receptive building principals, who were willing to commit to working with ANDRUS over a three-year grant cycle. The characteristics of each of these schools, gathered from 2013–2014 NYSED enrollment data, is briefly described below (schools are represented by pseudonyms).

P.S. 1A. P.S. 1A served 432 students in grades K–6 with a student body that was 89 percent Black, 8 percent Latino, 2 percent Asian, 0 percent White, and 0 percent multiracial, with 84 percent of its students eligible for free or reduced lunch, 4 percent designated as limited English proficient, and

14 percent designated for special education services. The school attendance rate was 92 percent, and a suspension rate of 7 percent was reported in 2013–2014.

P.S. 2A. P.S. 2A served 463 students in grades K–6 with a student population that was 85 percent Black, 13 percent Latino, 1 percent Asian, 1 percent White, and 1 percent multiracial, with 78 percent of students eligible for free or reduced lunch. Moreover, 10 percent of students were designated as limited English proficient, and 16 percent were designated for special education services. The school's attendance rate was 92 percent, and the state reported a suspension rate for 2013–2014 of 10 percent.

M.S. 3A. M.S. 3A served 517 students in grades 6–8. The students were 93 percent Black, 5 percent Latino, 0 percent Asian, 1 percent White, and 0 percent multiracial, with 76 percent eligible for free or reduced lunch. In addition, 2 percent of its students had been identified as limited English proficient and 27 percent designated for special education services. The school attendance rate was 94 percent, and the state reported a suspension rate for 2013–2014 of 17 percent.

M.S. 4A. M.S. 4A served 723 students in grades 7–8. Its student body was 71 percent Black, 21 percent Latino, 1 percent Asian, 7 percent White, and 0 percent multiracial, with 77 percent of the school's students eligible for free or reduced lunch. In M.S. 4A, 9 percent of its students were designated limited English proficient, and 23 percent were designated for special education services. The school attendance rate was 90 percent, and the reported suspension rate in 2013–2014 was 23 percent, according to the state.

P.S. 5B. P.S. 5B served 359 students from pre-K to grade 6 with a student body that was 54 percent Black, 38 percent Latino, 5 percent Asian, 1 percent White, and 1 percent multiracial, with 87 percent of students eligible for free or reduced lunch. P.S. 5B also had 8 percent of its students designated as limited English proficient and 20 percent designated for special education services. The school's attendance rate was 91 percent, and a suspension rate of 6 percent was reported by the state in 2013–2014. It is worth noting that this school, as a result of receiving a community-school grant, had a number of services not available at other project sites. These services, provided through ANDRUS, included the assignment of a licensed clinician to assume the role of community-school coordinator one day per week, a case manager to work with students and families four days per week, and two consultants to provide technical assistance and professional development throughout the year. These consultants also served as field researchers in collaboration with ANDRUS.

The Creating Sanctuary in Schools Project used a three-prong approach for all participants, including creating trauma-informed practices in schools, onsite technical assistance from Sanctuary Institute faculty and consultants, professional development workshops for all school personnel, and family engagement opportunities. To tackle the multitude of challenges involved with coordinating a public/private partnership of this magnitude, ANDRUS created the following structures and supports to facilitate project implementation at various levels.

Project Manager. The project manager, a senior member of the AN-DRUS Sanctuary Institute faculty, was assigned to oversee the Sanctuary initiative in District A. In this role, the director assigned ANDRUS faculty and consultants to work as a team with school faculty and support staff. She also had the very important responsibilities of facilitating communication among all stakeholders; supporting the work of the technical assistance teams; scheduling all grant-related activities; and, together with Sanctuary Institute faculty and school representatives, planning collaboratively and debriefing monthly. To conform to different grant guidelines and funding parameters, the role of coordination for District B unfolded somewhat differently and is described below.

Technical Assistance Teams. Teams assigned to project schools in District A consisted of approximately two to three ANDRUS Sanctuary Institute faculty with one member serving as the lead for coordinating the training and outreach to the principal. Members were randomly assigned to schools, based on their availability; however, in addition to ANDRUS faculty, two educational consultants were hired for the length of the grant to bring public school expertise to the work and facilitate cross-boundary knowledge and understanding. Collectively, these consultants had prior experience serving in a number of roles including that of classroom teacher, school administrator, community-school principal, and higher education faculty member. The educational consultants made use of their time in District B to disseminate the Sanctuary training afforded by ANDRUS and to take on the lead role of coordinating the community-school grant awarded to P.S. 5B.

P.S. 5B's site-based team for Sanctuary implementation consisted of the principal and ANDRUS's part-time community-school coordinator, the assigned caseworker, and onsite therapist. Additional support for this team came from ANDRUS's vice president for community-based programs and the two consultants charged with oversight of community-school grant implementation and field research.

PROFESSIONAL DEVELOPMENT

Professional development played a pivotal role in bringing the Sanctuary Model to project sites in both districts; the grant received by P.S. 5B required an additional layer of professional development around community schools. In District A, early-release or student nonattendance days were devoted to workshops conducted with groups of various sizes and configurations. These workshops, reaching all school personnel, consisted of modules reflecting specific Sanctuary tool-kit strategies designed for improving responses to student adversity, trauma, and chronic stress. An important corollary to the professional development they received on classroom strategies included the less tangible goal of increasing teachers' sense of empowerment or efficacy regarding their abilities and willingness to work with all students.

In District B, professional development sessions for P.S. 5B were shorter in duration but more frequent throughout the year. These sessions included community-schools' fundamentals training and an orientation to whole child education for faculty and support staff. Parallel training was also offered to ANDRUS's clinicians delivering services at the school site. Sanctuary training was customized to align with district and school priorities but deliberately designed to follow similar themes and content that had been covered in all other project schools.

As in any initiative, the role of the principal is critical to its success. Early on in the project, a concerted effort was made to support principals along each step of the implementation process. To that end, two important programmatic elements were instituted: monthly principals' networking dinners and an end-of-year retreat. These two functions served to build community among all members of the project and to provide opportunities for problem solving and the sharing of ideas and resources. Similar strategies were under consideration for P.S. 5B.

FAMILY ENGAGEMENT

Recognizing the importance of family engagement in the lives of children is a key component of trauma-informed care. To ensure that families were informed about Sanctuary work taking place at the schools, Sanctuary Institute faculty delivered parent workshops at open house and back-to-school night during initial project implementation. While these two events were hosted for each school in the project, some schools later sponsored additional workshops to introduce parents to the skills used in the classrooms.

RESEARCH DESIGN

A project study was conducted in order to assess the impact of the Creating Sanctuary in Schools Project on teachers and support staff in the spring of 2015. ANDRUS began the process of collecting various forms of descriptive data in the spring of 2015 with the IRB (Institutional Review Board) covered under the grant and thus, the authors' exemption from IRB approval. Grant-required data-collection activities were approved by each participating school district with additional data called for by ANDRUS to deepen their understanding of Sanctuary's impact.

The field study consisted of a mixed-method design triangulating data from classroom observations, teacher interviews, and survey responses. Quarterly reports, submitted by the school principal and lead Sanctuary Institute faculty members at each school site, included the number and descriptions of workshops and outreach activities that had been conducted. In addition, staff evaluations of related professional development were completed at the end of each session, and final staff surveys regarding classroom implementation of Sanctuary strategies were administered to inform the content and direction of this chapter. Final surveys were completed by teachers and instructional support staff (i.e., teaching assistants and instructional aides) in all project schools, and a small number of random classroom observations and interviews were conducted by the consultants at M.S. 3A and P.S. 5B. These two schools were selected for further study as a result of the willingness of the building principal and teachers to participate.

RESEARCH QUESTIONS

As part of the field study, ANDRUS was interested in obtaining information that would help answer the following questions critical to the successful integration of trauma-responsive schools and classrooms:

1. How had staff knowledge and attitudes about trauma grown or changed as a result of Sanctuary training?

2. How extensively had Sanctuary toolkit strategies been implemented in classrooms?
3. In what ways had newly acquired knowledge and understanding about trauma been further integrated as part of pedagogical practice through-out the day?

SELF-ASSESSMENT SURVEY RESULTS

Teachers and support staff at each of the five schools participating in the Creating Sanctuary in Schools Project completed the self-assessment survey online in the spring of 2015. A total of 193 survey responses were received and analyzed for each school. Although there were individuals in each of the project schools who did not respond to all 15 of the items included in the survey, the response rate to these items ranged from 52 percent to 86 percent in every school with the exception of P.S. 1A.

P.S. 1A showed a consistent rate of 48 percent in response to particular survey items related to three of several areas under examination including "Classroom Integration," "Classroom Management," and "Sanctuary Tool-Kit Strategies Implementation." The first and second of the survey items in which P.S. 1A had less than 50 percent of respondents reply involved the integration of the seven Sanctuary Commitments (nonviolence, emotional intelligence, democracy, social responsibility, open communication, commitment to social learning, and growth and change) as part of classroom instruction and within all social contexts of classroom life. The second area dealt with several facets of classroom management including incorporating Sanctuary's goals to promote self-regulation, caring and respectful relationships, and preserving student dignity; maintaining student expectations while providing flexible boundaries; and recognizing student efforts to manage their behavior. The third area makes reference to the implementation of specific Sanctuary tool-kit strategies. The writers of this chapter can only hypothesize about the reasons for the lower response rate by postulating, for example, that this might likely be attributed to a discomfort or hesitancy experienced by instructional staff in responding to questions about their own classrooms in relation to these three elements of professional practice.

As part of the survey, teachers and instructional support staff rated their own levels of application in terms of the professional development they had received over the course of two years in District A and one year in District B. Self-assessment ratings of either "Consistent Implementation" or "Full Implementation with Distinction" were used to identify the strongest areas of Sanctuary impact. Those rating themselves at "Moderate" and "Consistent" were used to identify "developing" elements of practice. The parameters for these ratings were based upon the expertise of the consultants, whose extensive experience in working with teachers led them to define "developing" practices as those "still in the process of adoption" because they fall short of "full implementation with distinction." Responses at levels designated "Beginning" or "Not There Yet" served to identify those elements of professional practice in which the Sanctuary Model has not thus far achieved a major impact.

Table 3.1 identifies all fifteen of the indicators of professional practice associated with the desired outcomes for full implementation of the Sanctuary Model in classrooms. Survey data from elementary project schools showed a solid trend in support of developing practices that are clearly aligned with the Sanctuary Model and an outcome of the professional development they have received.

Additional survey findings in table 3.2 identify the most salient indicators in which Sanctuary had a major impact on the practices of all elementary school respondents. Table 3.2 clearly shows that the Creating Sanctuary in Schools Project, at the time of this writing, was having its most "significant" impact at the elementary level. This finding was determined by the total, at or above 70 percent, who rated themselves at "Consistent" and "Fully Implementing" levels. Using this benchmark as a measure of significant impact, the following elements of professional practice appeared to be the most heavily influenced by the Sanctuary Model, regardless of whether these elementary schools were in their first or second year of implementation: Knowledge and Understanding, Classroom Interactions, and specific indicators or facets of Classroom Management.

In terms of project middle schools, these settings had the highest percentages of teachers and instructional support staff who rated themselves as "Not There Yet" or at a "Beginning" level of implementation. The data from these settings are presented in table 3.3, thereby plotting a course for future professional development and, most importantly, also suggesting that further dissemination of the Sanctuary Model to other schools at the secondary level pay particular attention to these specific indicators of professional practice. It should also be noted that the implementation of personal safety plans (strategies for promoting self-regulation and feelings of safety), intended for both teachers and students, remained at an initial phase of adoption during the

Table 3.1.   Elementary Survey Results Indicating Developing Practices of Sanctuary Model

Element of Professional Practice	Item Indicator of Developing Practice	Average of the Percent Totals at Moderate and Consistent Levels of Implementation
Knowledge and Understanding	Approaches to individual students are developmentally appropriate (i.e., taking into account the student's age, cognitive development, and emotional disposition).	73%
Knowledge and Understanding	Classroom practices reflect an understanding of the impact of chronic stress and adverse childhood experiences on learning.	77%
Classroom Interactions	Adults model interactions that promote a sense of belonging, self-esteem, and self-actualization.	74%
Classroom Interactions	Sanctuary concepts and vocabulary are integrated as part of classroom interactions.	76%
Classroom Interactions	The class is aligned with Sanctuary's tenets to provide an environment that is safe and inviting with a strong sense of community.	76%
Classroom Integration	Classroom displays reflect the implementation of Sanctuary Tool-Kit strategies.	72%
Classroom Integration	In my classroom, one or more of Sanctuary's 7 Commitments are integrated as part of classroom instruction.	76%
Classroom Integration	The 7 Sanctuary Commitments (Nonviolence, Emotional Intelligence, Democracy, Social Responsibility, Open Communication, Commitment to Social Learning, Growth and Change) are communicated as student expectations within all social contexts of classroom life.	73%

Classroom Management	Management strategies support an environment that is trauma informed by maintaining Sanctuary's 4 Domains of Safety (physical, moral, social, and emotional).	71%
Classroom Management	Expectations for student behavior emphasize self-regulation, caring and respectful relationships, and preserving student dignity.	67%
Classroom Management	Class rules governing student behavior preserve the civility of classroom interactions while providing boundaries for students who are flexible and trauma informed.	61%
Classroom Management	Adult members of the classroom routinely recognize student efforts to successfully manage and/or monitor their own behavior.	74%
Sanctuary Toolkit Strategies	I have created a personal Safety Plan and regularly model its use with students.	61%
Sanctuary Toolkit Strategies	Sanctuary Community Meetings are an established classroom routine.	53%
Assessment of Student Progress	In my classroom there is a system for assessing students' social-emotional growth and change over time.	75%

spring of 2015 in all project schools, according to the survey data. This is likely due to the complexity and sensitive nature of the Sanctuary training modules and the amount of time needed to fully realize each component of the training.

Variations in survey data results within project schools are also noteworthy. For example, although each of the project schools in District A had participated in the Creating Sanctuary in Schools Project for two years at the time of this writing, P.S. 5B appeared to have benefited from the additional services it received as a community school and from having a principal with a clinical background in social work. The formation of an onsite Sanctuary team, as described earlier, helped to facilitate post–professional development coaching and regular push-in support with all faculty and staff. Included in this support were many opportunities for modeling sanctuary approaches in classrooms and in other school spaces. Survey results at this school were thus comparable to project elementary schools in their second year of implementation. Furthermore, in relation to Sanctuary's community meeting strategy,

Table 3.2. Elementary School Survey Results Indicating Major Areas of Sanctuary Impact

Element of Professional Practice	Item Indicator of Successful Implementation	Average of the Percent Totals at Consistent and Fully Implemented with Distinction
Knowledge and Understanding	Classroom practices reflect an understanding of the impact of chronic stress and Adverse Childhood Experiences (ACE) on Learning.	70%
Classroom Interactions	Adults model interactions that promote a sense of belonging, self-esteem, and self-actualization.	80%
Classroom Interactions	The class is aligned with Sanctuary's tenets to provide an environment that is safe and inviting with a strong sense of community.	70%
Classroom Management	Class rules governing student behavior preserve the civility of class interactions while providing boundaries that are flexible and trauma informed.	75%
Class Management	Adult members of the classroom community routinely recognize student efforts to successfully manage and/or monitor their own behavior.	77%

P.S. 5B showed both the highest response rate to this survey item (82 percent) and the second highest percentage (65 percent) of those rating themselves at "Consistent" or "Fully" implementing levels.

RESULTS OF INTERVIEW DATA

To complement the survey and classroom-data collection, twenty-minute interviews were conducted with nine teachers, four representing P.S. 5B and five representing M.S. 3A. In P.S. 5B, the small interview sample represented a range of grade levels and class configurations including one first-grade teacher, one fifth-grade teacher, one self-contained upper-grade special-education class, one fourth-grade teacher, and one kindergarten teacher. At M.S. 3A, the sample included one Spanish teacher, two mathematics teachers, one special educator resource teacher and one English teacher. Interviewed

Table 3.3. Middle School Survey Results Indicating Areas of Limited Sanctuary Impact

School	Element of Professional Practice	Item Indicators of Limited Implementation	Percent Total: "Not There Yet" and "Beginning" Levels of Implementation
M.S. 3A M.S. 4A	Knowledge and Understanding	Approaches to individual students are developmentally appropriate.	33% 24%
M.S. 3A M.S. 4A	Knowledge and Understanding	Classroom practices reflect an understanding of the impact of chronic stress and adverse childhood experiences on learning.	21% 26%
M.S. 3A M.S. 4A	Classroom Interactions	Adults model interactions that promote a sense of belonging, self-esteem, and self-actualization.	22% 30%
M.S. 3A M.S. 4A	Classroom Interactions	Sanctuary concepts and vocabulary are integrated as part of classroom interactions.	40% 47%
M.S. 3A M.S. 4A	Classroom Interactions	The class is aligned with Sanctuary's tenets to provide an environment that is safe and inviting with a strong sense of community.	31% 46%
M.S. 3A M.S. 4A	Classroom Integration	Classroom displays reflect the implementation of Sanctuary Tool-Kit strategies.	52% 70%
MS 3A MS 4A	Classroom Integration	In my classroom, one or more of Sanctuary's 7 Commitments are integrated as part of classroom instruction.	33% 63%

MS 3A MS 4A	Classroom Interactions	The 7 Sanctuary Commitments (Nonviolence, Emotional Intelligence, Democracy, Social Responsibility, Open Communication, Commitment to Social Learning, Growth and Change) are communicated as student expectations within all social contexts of classroom life.	36% 44%
M.S. 3A M.S. 4A	Classroom Interactions	Management strategies support an environment that is trauma informed by maintaining Sanctuary's 4 Domains of Safety (physical, moral, social and emotional).	37% 36%
M.S. 3A M.S. 4A	Classroom Interactions	Expectations for student behavior emphasize self-regulation, caring and respectful relationships, and preserving student dignity.	23% 35%
M.S. 3A M.S. 4A	Classroom Interactions	Class rules governing student behavior preserve the civility of classroom interactions, while providing boundaries for students that are flexible and trauma informed.	22% 41%
M.S. 3A M.S. 4A	Classroom Interactions	Adult members of the classroom routinely recognize student efforts to successfully manage and/or monitor their own behavior.	Not Applicable 31%
M.S. 3A M.S. 4A	Classroom Integration	I have created a personal Safety Plan and regularly model its use with students.	38% 50%

M.S. 3A	Classroom	Sanctuary Community	37%
M.S. 4A	Integration	Meetings are an established classroom routine.	69%
M.S. 3A	Classroom	In my classroom there is	40%
M.S. 4A	Integration	a system for assessing students' social-emotional growth and change over time.	44%

teachers were randomly selected, with modifications based upon their willingness to participate and availability.

Interviews sought to deconstruct teachers' thinking about trauma and to better understand how they were applying the Sanctuary training to their classrooms. In order to gain a broader and deeper understanding of these two general areas of inquiry, the following interview questions were posed to teachers:

- How has your knowledge of child and human development, along with your ideas about trauma, changed?
- What insights have you gained as a result of your Sanctuary training?
- What type of practices are you implementing now that reflect Sanctuary's 7 Commitments or describe how your community meetings have been going?
- How has your ability to work more effectively with your students changed?
- If I walked into your classroom, what changes would I see as a result of Sanctuary?
- How have your professional practices and skills expanded as a result of Sanctuary training?
- In what ways has Sanctuary training about trauma impacted the school climate?

Data from the interviews were coded to capture themes embedded in the following elements of professional practice that were connected to the goals of the Creating Sanctuary in Schools Project. These elements included the teachers' knowledge of child/human development and trauma, their sense of efficacy in believing that they could work effectively with all students, and the implementation of a repertoire of professional skills and strategies linked either directly or indirectly to their Sanctuary training. A summary of interview responses is depicted in table 3.4.

Although it is difficult to generate any broad conclusions from the limited number of interviews conducted at two of the five project sites, the information yielded does provide some insights about teachers' perceptions that were also reflected in the results of the self-assessment surveys. In triangulating results with these survey findings, for example, the interview data also showed an overall increase in teachers' knowledge about trauma and its impact on students, as a result of Sanctuary training, with only two of the elementary teachers interviewed indicating that their knowledge of child development had remained unchanged. Perhaps these teachers felt that they had received an adequate level of teacher preparation in this area at the university level and, thus, did not view the information provided as having increased their knowledge base. Moreover, school-based professional development had primarily been focused on the improvement of academic performance, possibly resulting in the perception that this kind of training has less value.

As revealed through the interviews, an increase in teachers' awareness of trauma appeared to have been the result of gaining a fuller understanding of the causes of human behavior and an enhanced ability to choose appropriate interventions to counteract student misconduct. Furthermore, the majority of elementary respondents who had been interviewed at both schools indicated

Table 3.4.   Summary of Interview Responses

Elements of Practice	Interview Response Themes *n*=9
Demonstrated growth in knowledge about child/human development and trauma.	• More awareness of trauma (*n*=7) • More awareness of child development (*n*=2) • Insights about causes of behavior and use of appropriate interventions (*n*= 9) • Implementing tool-kit strategies (*n*=7)
Demonstrated growth in attitudinal shifts reflecting a greater sense of self-empowerment and self-efficacy about their abilities to reach their students.	• Working more effectively with students (*n*=9) • Changes in classroom interactions (*n*=4) • Increased sense of confidence (*n*=7) • Creating a positive classroom environment (*n*=4)
Demonstrated an expansion of professional skills in ways that meaningfully engage youngsters within broader contexts for learning.	• Increase repertoire of skills (*n*=6) • Positive changes in school climate (*n*=7)

that they had implemented community meetings, an important Sanctuary tool-kit strategy, with positive results for both individual students and the entire class. However, it should be noted that scheduling conflicts in M.S. 3A required that community meetings take place during designated advisory periods. Two elementary teachers stated,

> I am more aware of trauma and its stages. The training opened my eyes to kids' triggers. I know how to respond and be in tune with kids' feelings. The Community Meetings, using conversations about feelings, helps to set a positive tone for the day.

> I conduct Community Meetings in the morning. The meetings help students understand that I care about them so they share their feelings.

In terms of another, less tangible element of pedagogy focusing on attitudinal shifts among the teachers who had been interviewed, the teachers clearly articulated a greater sense of empowerment or belief in their ability to work more effectively with challenging students. This greater sense of confidence was reported by seven of the nine interviewees. A third elementary teacher responded,

> I have more skills now. I relate to students better. I can see when they are having a bad day and know it is time to stop and make them more aware of their feelings. I feel more confident and have other strategies to fall back on.

It is also interesting to note that although all teachers (n=9) reported an increased ability to work effectively with challenging students as a result of Sanctuary training, only the four elementary teachers who had been interviewed at P.S. 5B made specific reference to changes in their practice. In contrast, it appears that middle school teachers at M.S. 3A did not think that it was necessary to change any aspect of their classroom environment or their instruction. As is the case with many secondary educators, more of their efforts are focused on teaching content than in creating positive social interactions and nurturing social-emotional wellness. The results of both surveys and interviews communicate the importance of seeking balance between the two as a necessary prerequisite to achieving academic success.

In demonstrating an expansion of professional skills in ways that meaningfully engage youngsters within broader contexts for learning, two critical themes emerged with potential for school-wide impact. Four elementary teachers and two middle school teachers reported building a Sanctuary skill set to support students. Their described repertoire of skills included under-standing the impact of trauma on learning, identifying student triggers, im-plementing community meetings, having a greater awareness of student needs, and encouraging students to identify their feelings. These skills, em-bedded throughout the professional-development cycle presented by Sanctu-ary Institute faculty, are essential to good pedagogy and represent important foundational elements of the Sanctuary Model. Therefore, the data suggest that the sanctuary's clinical approaches can readily cross over into the arena of good instructional practice, provided that explicit connections are made for teachers and instructional support staff, along with practical methods for integration.

Seven of the nine teachers interviewed expressed the sentiment that changes were occurring in each building to create a positive school climate. They related this improvement to changes that allowed students to feel more connected to school and valued as individuals, to the improvement of their social skills and in everyone beginning to use Sanctuary to frame their think-ing. It is not surprising that Sanctuary's capacity to promote common under-standings, shared practices, and a common language seems to have a direct and positive impact on school culture and climate, an area worthy of explora-tion as part of future research.

RESULTS OF CLASSROOM OBSERVATIONS

A series of observations was conducted at P.S. 5B and M.S. 3A by ANDRUS consultants, each of whom had become familiar with the schools during workshop presentations, retreat dinners hosted for the principals by AN-DRUS, or, as in the case with P.S. 5B, working directly with faculty and staff to implement the community-school grant they had received. More than half of the classes were randomly selected for these informal visits. At P.S. 5B, observations included eight classrooms at various grade levels, including special education. At M.S. 3A, eight teachers (including special education) in grades 7–8 were observed teaching a variety of subjects. A number of these observations intentionally included principal recommendations based on their judgments of effective Sanctuary implementation. This selection pro-cess thus allowed the field researchers to gain insight into what principals considered effective sanctuary implementation.

The Classroom Observation Checklist examined similar indicators of pro-fessional practice to those in the self-assessment surveys and interviews. This checklist sought to observe elements of practice related to classroom interactions, environmental characteristics, and classroom management. Moreover, the teachers' efforts to integrate Sanctuary concepts and implement its tool-kit strategies were also studied. Classroom observations, although limited to providing a single snapshot of classrooms, seemed to demonstrate results somewhat similar to those of the survey and interviews already described. These observations showed a much higher number of teachers at P.S. 5B performing at "Accomplished" or "Exemplary" levels than those at the middle school in relation to the aforementioned indicators or elements of professional practice. However, it was not possible to draw any definitive conclusions about the implementation of Sanctuary tool-kit strategies due to the random timing of classroom observations throughout the school day. To allow for a closer examination of the integration of Sanctuary approaches and the implementation of specific tool-kit strategies, future classroom observations should be scheduled accordingly.

LIMITATIONS OF THE STUDY

Consistent with ANDRUS's reputation as an innovator in providing mental health services and in disseminating their successful approaches to public school settings, it is important to point out that attempts to gather documentation drawing from the clinical field of mental health and applying it to the field of education was also groundbreaking. The present chapter draws upon the strength of this type of analysis but clearly acknowledges its drawbacks in having, for example, limited time and access to school personnel already constrained by a tightly regulated school calendar. Moreover, this chapter is not intended to convey the parameters of a scientific investigation. Instead, it shares the perspectives gleaned from program insiders working with "real kids" participating in nonexperimental schools and classroom settings. Finally, this study does not include data pertaining to family-engagement activities conducted as part of the Sanctuary initiative.

Although not scientifically validated as a research instrument, the self-assessment survey for the Creating Sanctuary in Schools Project was specifically developed to obtain information related to the research questions presented. ANDRUS experts and consultants (field investigators) then designed classroom checklists and interview protocols to complement the survey and explore prototypes for future research. The data were then analyzed using descriptive statistics.

CONCLUSIONS AND RECOMMENDATIONS

Overall results of the data collected indicated that the professional development offered by Sanctuary Institute faculty and consultants had created deep and meaningful connections in relation to the following: increasing teacher knowledge and understanding about the impact of trauma and chronic stress on learning, improving the nature and quality of classroom interactions in response to these factors, reframing classroom management, and expanding strategies for student engagement by supporting strong social-emotional development.

The data thus demonstrate the importance of providing sustained professional development in efforts to advance the implementation of trauma-informed schools and classrooms. It is also evident from the data that school change aimed at creating trauma-informed schools will require differentiated learning experiences for teachers and instructional support staff, particularly for those working at secondary levels, along with the time and resources needed to work through the challenges of reframing school values, culture, and practices to more developmental and student strength–based approaches.

The analysis of data described in this chapter also serves to underscore the importance of the systems-wide approach employed by Sanctuary in bringing to the forefront of our attention those nonacademic factors that weigh heavily on students' abilities to learn, including, for example, their capacity to self-regulate behavior, to listen and attend, and to adequately execute brain functions. This systems-wide approach was clearly reflected in the data that demonstrated emerging improvements in the school climate and culture of participating schools.

The current investigation underscores a number of implications for educators planning to implement trauma-informed schools and classrooms. Creating explicit connections between training content and its relationship to instructional practice and all aspects of life in classrooms should be foremost in the dissemination of a clinical model, such as Sanctuary, to classroom settings. The following recommendations are thus essential when one is asking teachers to consider the impact of trauma and the social-emotional domain of human development as an integral component of students' growth and learning:

• Providing teachers with a broader and deeper understanding of the impact of chronic levels of trauma, stress, and adversity on their students and on themselves, both personally and within the workplace, with a focus on professional development that has direct applications to classroom practice and integration with curriculum content.

- Affording teachers opportunities to practice their newly acquired trauma-responsive approaches including instructional strategies that teach and promote pro-social values, like those reflected in the seven Sanctuary Commitments, and an assets-based framework to promote problem-solving and solution-seeking behaviors. Ideally, these opportunities would be enacted with in-class coaching support and feedback from those with experience in the field of mental health and from other school colleagues who have shared in this special professional development experience.

- Examining broader implications of trauma-responsive approaches to include all aspects of classroom organization, interactions, and management, with a focus on intrinsic motivation, the management of emotions, and a respect for students' voices in ways that engender a sense of self-determination, empowerment, and a positive orientation toward their futures.

- Developing methods to effectively monitor student progress that include pro-social learning outcomes in which students have shared responsibility for establishing and monitoring goals and objectives that are relevant to their experiences both in and out of school. Individual goals, for example, might include students tracking the frequency they have avoided engaging in personal conflicts with classmates. At the classroom level, class members could monitor their collective ability to offer support to one another by acknowledging specific examples of this support at the end of each day or week in an open forum or class meeting.

- Establishing the importance of maintaining both a trauma-responsive classroom and school-wide approaches that are aligned and mutually supportive of one another. Furthermore, acting as a trauma-informed organization should secure "a place of honor" among other school-wide initiatives and be prioritized accordingly.

Given the current national focus on student test performance and school accountability, this chapter refocuses our attention on the importance of addressing chronic levels of trauma, stress, and adversity as integral components of whole-child education that are critical to student success and strong human growth and development. This approach requires the kind of public/private partnership that will facilitate the cross-system thinking and resource allocation described in this chapter.

Finally, the current investigation begins to show support for the community school strategy as both an efficient and logical way to garner, organize, and deliver the services and resources needed for supporting children and youth in ways that will also serve to improve outcomes for the entire school community.

By its very design, the Sanctuary Model not only serves to advance our understanding regarding the impact of adverse childhood experiences on learning but also serves to advance widely recognized "best practices in instruction" described by renowned experts in the field of curriculum, instruction, and teacher evaluation (i.e., Danielson, 1996; Dufour, Dufour, & Eaker, 2008; Tomlinson, 2003). This chapter highlights the need for leaders from the fields of mental health and education to further articulate this convergence and, in doing so, to provide yet another pathway for helping members of their respective professional communities to cross the boundaries of knowledge and approaches that have historically served to isolate their work from one another.

REFERENCES

Berliner, D. (2006, June 1). How poverty affects the changing suburbs in the northeast. Paper presented at The Changing Suburbs Institute Conference at Manhattanville College, Purchase, New York.

Bloom, S. L. (2011). *The Sanctuary Model*. Retrieved from http://www.sanctuaryweb.com/trauma-informed-systems.php.

Danielson, C. (1996). *Enhancing professional practice: A framework for teaching.* Alexandria, VA: Association for Supervision and Curriculum Development.

Dufour D., Dufour, R., & Eaker, R. (2008). *Revisiting professional learning communities at work.* Bloomington, IN: Solution Press.

Santiago, E., Ferrara, J., & Quinn, J. (2012). *Whole child, whole school: Applying theory to practice in a community school.* Lanham, MD: Rowman & Littlefield Education.

Tomlinson, C. (2003). *Fulfilling the promise of the differentiated classroom: Strategies and tools for responsive teaching.* Alexandria, VA: Association for Supervision and Curriculum Development.

Chapter Four

On Slavery and the Racialization of Teaching Practices

Jon N. Hale

Racially motivated acts of murder and terror in the tragic shooting in Charleston, South Carolina, in 2015, the "Unite the Right" rally in Charlottesville, Virginia, in 2017, and other such acts have spurred a national movement to address racial discrimination in our schools and classrooms. Within this movement is a demand to make race a central part of our social and political understandings and, therefore, educators are called upon to incorporate the study and discussion of race into our systems of education in meaningful ways. This can first be addressed by rooting out the racism in American curriculum, which is perpetuated by poorly executed curricular interventions within a larger context that is often unsupportive of teaching about race. The call to include race in the curriculum (Blum, 2012; Delpit, 2006; Emdin, 2016; Ladson-Billings, 2009; Lam, 2015; Milner, 2008, 2015; Valenzuela, 1999; Williams, Williams, & Blain, 2016) should begin with an examination of the litany of incidents in which race is evident in the classroom.

Numerous incidents of offensive race-based teaching that resulted in dismissal or reprimand have captured the attention of educators in this "postracial" era. These moments illustrate a paradox, highlighting that racism and racial ignorance are significant factors in contemporary education, though many claim that race is an insignificant category or deny the existence of virulent racism. In Ohio, a social studies teacher taught a lesson about the slave trade by reenacting a slave auction in the classroom. A black student played the role of the slave as the white students bid on their peer. The teacher was summarily dismissed. A teacher in New York bound the hands and feet of two black students in class in a lesson on slavery. Another teacher in Georgia resigned after writing offensive questions about slavery as part of a math homework assignment. Also in Georgia, students were asked to identify the negative *and positive* aspects of slavery. Other teachers in Georgia and Nevada permitted students to wear Ku Klux Klan robes as part of class projects and homework. A teacher in Florida allowed students to wear yellow Stars of David as part of a "Jew for a Day" lesson. In New York, yet another teacher permitted students to adopt the perspective of a member of the Nazi Party in a writing assignment (Chapelfield Elementary, 2011; Katrandjian, 2012; "KKK Robes," 2013; Flood, 2012; Thomas, 2018; Webley, 2011; Walker, 2010). These instances point to a mixed truth about the work of teachers, but particularly social studies educators. Teachers are incorporating racist and anti-Semitic history including slavery and the Holocaust, which are important topics to cover. However, instances of inappropriate teaching illustrate major shortcomings in how educators discuss race and the resultant need for greater scrutiny and more humane teaching practices.

In the wake of racial terror, educators, historians, and education researchers have pointed toward a deeper issue of racial ignorance and discrimination in our schools, examining how, for instance, educators largely fail to teach slavery as the cause of the Civil War or examine the history of racial violence that the long civil rights movement sought to eradicate (Anderson, 2018; "Civil Rights Movement Education Remains 'Woefully Inadequate,'" 2014; Jeffries, Blight, & Shuster, 2018; Theoharis, 2018; Turner, 2018). In the midst of ongoing racial disparities and discrimination and a growing movement to address them, educators and schools continue to fall short in effectively teaching a history of race and racism in the United States and the contemporary manifestations of this longer history.

Racist incidents in the classroom and a concomitant record of woefully teaching a race-based curriculum tell us that teachers are teaching about race or are implementing a race-based curriculum. This challenges a prevailing notion that educators are not incorporating race into the classroom. Moreover, those who are executing well-intentioned but harmful lessons are employing effective teaching methods and pedagogy. Therefore, a sharp disconnect exists between the intention to include race in the curriculum and the application of these ideas within the classroom. This research examines the role of teacher education programs in universities by interrogating the disconnect between theory and practice evident in these examples. Through an analysis of the intellectual trajectory and intersection of race, pedagogical theory, and practice within teacher education programs, this research explains how teachers understand the importance of race but mostly fail to grasp its pedagogical implications. Therefore, this article examines the origins of race-based curriculum found in institutions of higher learning that influence teaching in the public schools. These well-intentioned teachers taught topics connected to race in very problematic ways, but ones that were still grounded in highly regarded student-centered and kinesthetic activities based on culturally relevant topics. This pedagogy is grounded within the framework of progressivism, constructivism, multicultural education, and critical pedagogy adopted by many colleges of education. Though such practices constitute the canon of education theory and pedagogy, they lead to problematic discussions of race that preclude much-needed, structured, and genuine discussions about race without appropriate professional development.

Examining teacher education programs through an interpretive lens illuminates the significant role of race in the K–12 classroom. The methodological framework for this research is grounded in an interpretive and historical analysis focusing on the pedagogical canon, which consists of progressive education, constructivism, multicultural education, and critical pedagogy. This intellectual trajectory defines the pedagogical context in which the aforementioned incidents occurred. An interpretive and analytic framework is then used to examine a total of ten teacher education programs of representative institutions drawn from each of the six states in which the teaching under examination occurred: Ohio, New York, Florida, Georgia, Virginia, and Nevada. Data collection from these representative institutions focuses on curricular material including department and program mission statements, faculty curriculum vitae, program requirements, course descriptions, and syllabi. This material was analyzed for the occurrences, depth, and frequency of race, diversity, multiculturalism, and culturally relevant teaching within these sources. These themes demonstrate the extent to which race is incorporated throughout these teacher education programs.

This research reveals that teachers are receiving a progressive training in pedagogy, but a disconnect is precipitated by overarching concepts of "diversity," which in practice unfolds as an umbrella term that only potentially includes a systematic analysis of race. This research suggests that teacher education programs effectively instill a critical interpretation of education and race, but colleges of education fall short in fundamentally engaging issues of race and discrimination in their curriculum, overall missions, and, most importantly, in practice without appropriate professional development and oversight in the schools. Instances of racist and harmful teaching illustrate this complex disconnect. A lack of preparation and discussion at the institutional levels (teacher education programs, professional development, school district policy) create the space for well-intentioned educators to teach standards that discuss issues of race and discrimination, including slavery. Moreover, while representative teacher education programs teach about race, newly minted teachers enter a hostile climate that does not encourage professional discourse around race, which precludes the support needed to incorporate race into our classrooms. Without appropriate and ongoing professional development that examines white supremacy and helps deepen our understandings of race and racism, unethical and harmful teaching practices will continue to occur.

THEORY, PEDAGOGY, AND THE MARGINALIZATION OF RACE

Incidents of harmful teaching practices such as those related to race are grounded in research-based practices that make up a pedagogical canon within teacher education. The teachers who had students act out the slave auction or who allowed Ku Klux Klan robes in the classroom, for example, adopted an effective *form* of teaching, namely, pedagogy and instruction based on the interests and needs of students. The process of acting out and role playing in education is a common practice, even among some university professors. These practices, rooted in more ethical teaching, are data driven, with deep origins in the history of teacher education. Education based on experience and student-centered learning has constituted a "progressive" paradigm since the 1930s. However, these instances also illustrate a problematic disconnect between notions of race and professional and ethical teaching.

One of the major philosophies these practices are grounded in can be traced to John Dewey and pervasive notions of "progressive education" ubiquitously grounded in teacher education programs across the country. One of Dewey's core principles is the belief that "the only true education comes through the stimulation of the child's powers by the demands of the social situations in which he finds himself" (Dewey, 1897, p. 77). This formed a core body of knowledge for his work, which he expounded upon later in his career. "The fundamental unity of the newer philosophy," Dewey wrote in

1938 in reference to the thriving paradigm of progressive education, "is found in the idea that there is an intimate and necessary relation between the processes of actual experience and education" (Dewey, 1938, p. 20). However he was used in the classroom, he inspired a movement of progressive education that delineates a social realm necessary to effective teaching. The social realm of the student and the experience therein constitutes an important aspect of this philosophy, which is central to common practices in today's classrooms.

Dewey's work has been interpreted and misinterpreted in numerous ways since his seminal essay, "My Pedagogic Creed," in the late nineteenth century. As most foundations of education or philosophy of education courses imply, a thorough examination of Dewey in them is precluded for programmatic reasons. Therefore, a standard interpretation is often put forth. This has led to an interpretation that situated hands-on and student-centered learning that reconceptualizes knowledge production in terms of inquiry, discovery, and "natural" learning suited to the needs of the student. Dewey argued that the schools were of instrumental importance in that they "should take up and continue the activities with which the child is already familiar in the home . . . it should exhibit these activities to the child, and reproduce them in such ways that the child will gradually learn the meaning of them, and be capable of playing his own part in relation to them" (Dewey, 1897, p. 78). If the educators mentioned above had studied Dewey in more detail, his work *Experience and Education* would have made it clear that *experience* is not in and of itself positive or beneficial. As he makes clear, "the trouble is not the absence of experience, but their defective and wrong character" (Dewey, 1938, p. 27). Without deeper examination of activity and experience in the classroom, well-intentioned teachers can make poor decisions about what constitutes a legitimate activity.

Sociocultural theories of learning built upon Dewey and provided a new focus on the role of society and culture that was used in the education of young people. Students inherit a multitude of cues from their environment, such theories contended, including language and discourse. Children's culture and environment play a crucial role in their development. Sociocultural theorists, most notably the Russian psychologist Lev Vygotsky, introduced purposefully yet skillfully placed tasks to facilitate intellectual development. "The most significant moment in the course of intellectual development, which gives birth to the purely human forms of practical and abstract intelligence," Lev Vygotsky contended, "occurs when speech and practical activity . . . converge." In addition to the development of social interaction, Vygotsky advocated the use of play in furthering the development through a longer process. He went on to write that "a condition is reached in which the child begins to act independently of what he sees. . . . The freedom of action adults and more mature children enjoy is not acquired in a flash but has to go through a *long process of development*" (Vygotsky, 1978, pp. 24, 97). These social and cultural cues build upon the trajectory of Dewey, who argued for the "natural" development of young people through experience. Moreover, as students are pushed into "zones of proximal development" through cognitively difficult tasks, students acquire higher order thinking skills. The significance of such theories continues to readapt the role of both students and teachers, yet along the same lines as Dewey's student-centered pedagogy. By following the zones of proximal development, students are still naturally inquisitive, and teachers carefully select activities that push optimal development.

The work of constructivist thinkers in the latter part of the twentieth century continued to advance the intellectual trajectory of pedagogy predicated upon experience, society, and culture. Constructivism is the most recent point of entry experienced by students graduating from teacher education programs. One of the key assumptions of constructivism is the interplay between individual structures and culture (Fosnot, 1996, pp. 25–27). It also extends the trajectory of student-centered activity with origins in the Progressive Era. Constructivism is also based on issues or, ideally, problems that are relevant to the student. Yet, as in Vygostsky, students ultimately push through on their own with skillfully placed tasks or questions at pivotal moments. Constructivist advocates suggest that "constructivist teachers engage students in experiences that might engender contradictions to their initial hypotheses and then encourage discussion" (Brooks, 1996, p. 112). Moreover, advocates also call for "authenticity and context" (Brooks, 1996, p. 96). Topics within history and social studies, as observed, lend themselves to a constructivist methodology, which in turn leads to strong and effective teaching. This constitutes the most recent wave of examining how students construct their understanding of the world around them. The three schools of thought logically extend from one another to create a nearly linear development that is the foundation of the canon in teacher education. Yet as much as constructivism encourages teachers to base instruction on students interests and suppositions, hypotheses, and so on, it does not call for a specific racialized understanding of "controversy" among teachers.

As much as this philosophy shapes contemporary understandings of pedagogy, this form of thinking can be criticized for its blatant omission of race and derogatory stereotypes. John Dewey, for instance, is painfully ignorant of notions of "the other." When establishing the parameters of a (Western) society that depended upon education, Dewey claimed:

> Every one of the constituent elements of a social group, in a modern city as in a savage tribe, is born immature, helpless, without language, beliefs, ideas, or social standards. (Dewey, 1916, p. 2)

Dewey should be criticized for a lack of race consciousness and a reliance on terms like "savage" to articulate his philosophical arguments, as it signifies problematic conceptions of "the other" deeply embedded in the progressive canon. In this way, progressive education in terms of race can be anything but "progressive" (Fallace, 2011).

The race-neutral (at best) or racist assumptions that underpinned the pedagogical canon of progressivism and constructivism highlight an obvious shortcoming of "progressive" education. An analysis of the historical context of the work within progressivism and constructivism finds that students' interests and identities were factors when shaping curriculum and pedagogical development. But there is minimal evidence that the cultural strengths of students of color were considered in its construction. This pedagogical paradigm is predicated predominantly upon the needs of white students, as opposed to the diverse groups that populate the United States. Still today, mandates such as standardizing the curriculum, for instance, continue to exercise a form of de-racialization (Brown, 2007; Darling-Hammond, 2007). Standardizing allows teachers and teacher educators the opportunity to deal with race as, more or less, a checklist item that takes a break from content and curriculum, but instead placed in advisory coursework when discussing educational issues or trivialized by using it as a lesson when teaching students' similarities and differences.

This shortsightedness served as a catalyst for the turn toward multiculturalism, a theory of culture and education that constituted a significant awakening in teacher education programs by the turn of the twenty-first century. Contrary to the tendency toward de-racialization and dealing with race as a checklist item are multicultural education and culturally responsive teaching, two approaches that acknowledge racial and cultural identity as assets to learning. Neoliberalism negates the potential impact of these approaches by supporting a one-size-fits-all curriculum and providing best practices that focus on procedural steps and ignore the importance of encouraging a belief system (Hachfeld et al., 2015; Matias, 2013; Sleeter, 2012).

Multicultural education arose during the civil rights movement of the 1960s and 1970s, and it demanded an analysis of education that examined culture, race, and diversity. Multicultural education is a school-reform movement that emphasizes giving all students a chance to learn (Banks, 1995) and sees diversity as an educational and political strength. James Banks (1995), education theorist and scholar, developed five overlapping dimensions of multicultural education: content integration, the knowledge-construction process, prejudice reduction, an equity pedagogy, and an empowering school culture and social structure. Content integration describes ways teachers use more than one cultural perspective to teach key concepts and generalizations (Atwater et al., 2013; Banks, 1995). It challenges the teacher to go beyond the textbook that primarily provides one meaning, explanation, and articulation of a concept. It embraces multiple perspectives and the nuances of those perspectives, and it introduces students to multiple entries to processing and understanding. During the knowledge-construction process, the teacher facilitates and guides the students to not simply accept knowledge for what it is, but to inquire into deeper meanings and understandings. Teachers help students investigate the frames of reference, perspectives, and biases that influence the ways in which knowledge is constructed (Banks, 1995; Sarraj et al., 2015). The prejudice-reduction dimension relates to students' racial attitudes and teachers' strategies to develop democratic values.

Some schools of education challenged supremacy more assertively through critical pedagogy. Through the teaching of critical pedagogy, educators seek to promote critical thinking in the interest of social change for all people, to name and identify oppression in order to change it, and to recognize a link between knowledge, power, and oppression. The theory and practice reveal how social, political, and economic relationships are distorted and manipulated through the politics and dynamics of power, privilege, and supremacy. Education is therefore conceptualized through a critical lens to embrace larger social justice projects and to address institutional discrimination, including white supremacy, in the curriculum (Darder, 2011; Freire, 2002; hooks, 1994; Lam, 2015).

In essence, prejudice reduction pushes against "White bias" (Banks, 1995; Allen, Scott, & Lewis, 2013). The assumption is that although the United States espouses democratic values, the American educational system constructs, manages, disseminates, and supports learning from a position of white supremacy and privilege, which ultimately normalizes students' understanding of knowledge and narrows the opportunity for any group that is not white to be considered primary. In truth, we know that democratic values are about freedom and equality for all. Equity pedagogy happens when teachers make use of their cultural competence to modify their teaching to intentionally reference and make use of students' skills, experiences, and competencies. The assumption is that academic achievement can be increased when teaching strategies are built on referential connections to students' culture (Banks, 1995; Bennett, 2013; Bondy et al., 2012; hooks, 1994). Although it is assumed that what works for white students will also work for students of color, race and ethnicity matter when it comes to maximizing learning outcomes for students from diverse backgrounds (Hawley & Nieto, 2010; Whipp, 2013). Teaching and learning are influenced in two ways by race and ethnicity: they influence how students respond to instruction, and they influence teachers' assumptions about how students learn (Hawley & Nieto, 2010; Shevalier & McKenzie, 2012).

An empowering school culture and social structure view the school as a complex system that must be restructured in order to effectively reform schools (Banks, 1995). School structures affect students' opportunities to learn, and in schools with race-responsive school cultures, teachers and administrators focus on their students and the experiences they bring with them (Gooden & O'Doherty, 2015; Hawley & Nieto, 2010; Knaus, 2014). This dimension speaks to reform sustainability that creates opportunity to see change not just with one teacher or one school but also as an entire system. Multicultural education informs educational practice and magnifies dimensions to take a closer look at the intricacies that influence education. Culturally responsive teaching continues the exploration by bringing us closer to educational practice.

Culturally responsive teaching uses ethnically diverse students' cultural characteristics and experiences to develop engaging and effective lessons (Gay 2002, 2013; Griner & Stewart, 2012; Gist, 2014). The response is influenced by a belief system that all students can be successful and pertains to using culturally based strategies to produce positive academic and social outcomes within and beyond the school. Teachers help students to understand that knowledge has political and moral elements, and students are empowered to construct meaning, examine what they are learning, and challenge the status quo (Gay, 2002; Harmon, 2012; Martell, 2013; Milner, 2015; Warren, 2013). Contrary to many traditional classrooms, controversial issues related to race, class, and ethnicity are welcomed and addressed. Ultimately, students are groomed to become contributing adults who are socially conscious change agents. Learning to teach to and through students' strengths creates a foundation built on sincere and authentic relationships between teacher and student.

At the moment of a stronger demand for race in the curriculum, this research identifies strong teacher-education preparation and sound pedagogical and instructional preparation. Race is subsumed in this larger context, which is in part shaped by larger social and political demands for diversity and multiculturalism. This is contested, and when race is included in the pedagogical milieu of "diversity," this form of teaching becomes unclear to teachers who are theoretically prepared in these issues but lack ongoing professional and social support for teaching them. This chapter therefore illuminates the disconnect between preparation and classroom practice and identifies this moment of praxis as a critical juncture in the movement toward more equitable education by way of a race-based curriculum.

THE FUNCTION OF RACE IN TEACHER EDUCATION PROGRAMS

Racial issues have historically plagued the United States' principles of democracy, freedom, justice, and equality. Institutions of higher learning have challenged such issues by standing as beacons of enlightenment and intellectualism. Teacher educators in colleges and schools of education across the nation profess to students with the hopes that societies' intellectual capital will grow, oppressive beliefs will cease, and the American educational system will succeed. This creed is evident in the intellectual trajectory of teacher education programs throughout the twentieth century. Yet when confronted with instances of harmful race-based teaching, a disconnect with teacher education programs emerges (Buehler et al., 2009; Ullucci & Battey, 2011). Clearly, teacher education does not prepare teachers to be ignorantly racist. Based on college mission statements, programs of study, and faculty research agendas, there is a great deal of evidence that race and racial issues are being addressed but mostly as part of discussions around the topic of diversity. This praxis of "diversity" illustrates an institutional imperfection that engenders strong objectives but mediocre and, at times, harmful practices in the classroom.

One of the most striking features of teacher education programs in a context of race is a common and public commitment to diversity. Indeed, sixty years after the *Brown v. Board of Education* decision in 1954 and the birth of the modern civil rights movement, schools of education play great homage to diversity. This is most often evident in programs, departments, and education colleges' mission statements. At the Curry School of Education at the University of Virginia, for instance, the school "values diversity in all of its complexity and richness. We engage our students with multiple perspectives to prepare them to be active agents of change" (UVA, "Diversity at Curry," 2018). The first principle in the mission statement at the University of Nevada, Reno, is similarly committed to diversity, or, "to develop and strengthen the capacity of educators to serve an increasingly linguistically and ethnically diverse student population in ways so that each student is successful" (UNV-R, "About Us," 2015). The mission statement for the Department of Educational Theory and Practice at the University of Georgia espouses a commitment and passion to improve the world through community engagement (UGA, "About the College," 2015). Syracuse University adopts a mission statement explicitly devoted to diversity, and claims:

> [Syracuse is] a national leader in improving and informing educational practice for diverse communities, is committed to the principle that diverse learning communities create the conditions that both enrich the educational experience and provide opportunities for all to succeed. (Syracuse, "Course Catalog," 2015)

Syracuse also pioneered the inclusion movement in the United States, which was influential in framing learning in a way for students to participate fully in mainstream classrooms and other inclusive learning environments.

Such mission statements indicate a public and shared commitment to diversity and programmatic goals and are often built around it. The standard teacher education program supports diversity and multicultural education; however, it occurs mostly in upper-level, graduate, or specified programs. The Ohio State University College of Education and Human Ecology has developed a five-year diversity plan that calls for the director of each school to create an equity and diversity committee to carry out diversity initiatives (OSU, "Multicultural and Equity Studies in Education," 2015). Teaching and Learning, one of three departments of the College of Education, has seven specializations, and one of the seven is "Multicultural and Equity Studies in Education." The Multicultural and Equity Studies in Education program is for students interested in studying identities and inequalities associated with race, class, gender, ethnicities, and sexualities in education (OSU, "Multicultural and Equity Studies in Education," 2015). Courses within this program include "Multicultural and Global Perspective on Teaching and Learning," "Teaching about Latin America and Latin American Perspectives," and "International Perspectives on Educational Equity and Diversity."

The University of Georgia offers a graduate certificate in diversity, equity, and inclusion in education, which is offered as a nondegree program. The fifteen-hour course covers issues related to race, socioeconomics, sexual orientation, and gender identity. Overall, the students are expected to develop a deeper understanding of systemic oppression. The coursework emphasizes the interdisciplinary nature of diversity by exploring foundations of psychology, sociology, political economy, history, and culture of diversity (UGA, "Certificate in Diversity," 2015). Because there are minimal degree offerings specifically related to multicultural education, and mostly offered as certification, it would suggest that what is needed to become a highly effective teacher is separate from what is needed to become a highly effective multicultural-education teacher. But the College of Education's position on preparing students to develop culturally relevant curriculum speaks to the depth and awareness of the importance of being able to make connections with students who may be marginalized or fail to fit into the mainstream.

The College of Education at Florida Atlantic University has seven departments that touch upon diversity in course content and requirements. The Department of Teaching and Learning and the Department of Curriculum, Culture, and Educational Inquiry both emphasize multicultural education and diversity (FAU, "Department of Curriculum," 2015). It offers the "Introduction to Diversity for Educators" course, which requires a fifteen-hour field component. In addition, the students are required to take twenty-four hours of social science content. Six of those hours must be chosen from four options: "Race and Ethnic Relations," "Global Inequality and Crisis," "Poverty and Society," and "Gender and Equity." This coursework, including the fifteen-hour field component, demonstrates preparation to work with a diverse group of impoverished students (FAU, "Department of Curriculum," 2015). The curriculum at Syracuse University requires that three of the sixteen required credit hours in the core courses cover diversity, for social studies teachers, and four of twenty-seven credit hours that deal directly with diversity. Even in these courses, it is not guaranteed that race is covered (Syracuse, Social Studies BA, 2015).

The Masters of education in curriculum and instruction at Florida Atlantic University addresses issues of diversity and develops students' global perspective on education. Students are required to take "Global Perspectives of Curricular Trends across Nations" or "Foundations of Global Education," as well as an online multicultural-education K–12-specialization course (FAU, "Master of Education in Curriculum," 2018). If one is pursuing an educational specialist degree (EdS) in curriculum and instruction, the "Race, Class and Gender Issues in Education" course is one of six options, and "Mathematical Multicultural Education Reading" is an option as an area of specialization (FAU, "Education Specialist Degree," 2018). The Department of Teaching and Learning offers a master's degree (EdM) in elementary education with ESOL plus certification that requires students to take the "Education in a Multicultural Society" course. An EdM in curriculum and instruction requires students to take the "Introduction to Diversity for Educators" course, which includes a fifteen-hour field component, and an EdM in environmental education, which requires "Foundations of Global Education or Global Perspectives of Curricular Trends" (FAU, "Master's Degree in Environmental Education," 2018).

Programs at Florida Atlantic University, Ohio State University, the University of Georgia, and the University of Washington also offer upper-level and graduate courses specifically on multicultural education and diversity. Quite notably, these institutions examined the social context of education, which connects this topic to the longer tradition supported by progressive education and sociocultural learning theories. The University of Virginia is another institution that teaches about multiculturalism in upper-level and graduate courses, in courses on social issues. For example, the course description of a social studies methods course required at the University of Virginia mentions that students study "historical content: standards and accountability, curriculum/unit/lesson planning, engaging approaches for the teaching of history, assessment in the social studies and multiculturalism" (UVA, EDIS 5600, "Teaching Social Studies in the Secondary School," 2015).

Although the titles and descriptions of programs of study fail to point out the level of depth each identity and associated inequality will be given during the course, the opportunities to explore in-depth issues related to multicultural education are largely limited to the upper level. Moreover, some schools of education, in fact, provide exemplary content grounded in race. The University of Virginia and Syracuse University, for example, both offer a degree in cultural foundations of education. African American studies is one of nine social science areas. Such course offerings provide disciplinary analysis. Courses on the foundations of education, the history of education, the American school, and others are based in the conceptual and intersectional analysis of education, which draws from the disciplines of history, philosophy, sociology, anthropology, and others to define, discuss, and contextualize race. Such course offerings also indicate a strong faculty interest in the examination of race. Faculty at these institutions maintain active research agendas and teaching interests in, for instance, historical construction of race, migration, transnationalism, Latina/o history, community and school relations, and the formation of urban schools (Syracuse, "Faculty," 2018). At the University of Virginia, one faculty member studied the twentieth-century history of African American schooling in the South before mandated desegregation and closely examined how educational history informs current schooling policy and practice (UVA, "Faculty," 2018). Other scholars hold impressive credentials and, in the field of social studies education, earned awards from the National Council for the Social Studies (NCSS) and published on the historical thinking in relation to state standards. In these instances, race or diversity is not always reflected in course tittles or descriptions. However, faculty research interests indicate a strong familiarity and mastery of racial analysis that can easily be incorporated into the classroom. Several faculty members have expertise in areas such as critical race theory, critical multiculturalism, black feminist theory, and Latino critical race theory. The expertise of the faculty is therefore a good indicator of course direction and emphasis.

Students are unquestionably exposed to or have the opportunities to study race directly before they reach upper-level courses in education. Students take such courses outside of education departments, most often in schools of social science or humanities. This line of study is required among social studies–education majors. More than likely, students draw content from other course requirements. In the case of the University of Nevada, Reno, one ethnic/diversity course (three hours) is required in the social sciences for all majors (UNV-R, "General Catalog," 2015). Also common is a general requirement without the qualifications of diversity. Like these programs, the candidates' understanding of race and multiculturalism comes from the students' content area in history. The humanities include literature, fine arts, or moral philosophy, foreign language and religious perspectives, history, anthropology, economics, politics, psychology, sociology, African American studies, linguistics, and studies in women and gender (UVA, "College of Arts & Sciences," 2015). The inclusion of race, of course, depends on the extent to which race and "diversity" are taught by the instructors, which points to the fact that colleges of education are dependent upon the disciplines for this content knowledge before taking upper-level courses in education.

Race, however, is predominantly absent or, at best, subsumed under topics of diversity. Programmatic commitment to diversity is common in teacher education programs, but an analysis of program requirements reveals that diversity does not necessarily include race. In the case of Syracuse University, for instance, diversity can be defined linguistically or behaviorally, but not necessarily by race. This program also illustrates how "urban" studies can serve as a euphemism for broad conceptions of diversity as well. This institution provides content specific to urban education through a lecture series that is "dedicated to the presentation of current ideas and strategies for navigating urban education terrain in the United States" (Douglas P. Biklen Landscape of Urban Education Lecture Series). Like diversity, however, "urban" studies programs hold the potential to preclude a serious discussion of race.

The University of Nevada, Reno, also illustrates the multifarious nature of "diversity." This institution defines diversity through teaching students with disabilities, in this particular case, students with disabilities in a general-education classroom. The program's introductory class includes this objective: "Students will be able to identify cultural, racial, and gender differences and how these differences relate to education and society as a whole through systematic discussions" (UNV-R, "General Catalog," EDU 202). Another requirement of secondary social studies majors is "Education for a Changing World," which includes the objective of examining "multicultural issues within a broad sociocultural context, focusing on cultural frames of reference for understanding" (UNV-R, "General Catalog," EDU 412). This program provides an exemplar of national programs in teacher education. However, while striving for inclusiveness, the conceptual approach fails to address race and its implications; even connections to stronger analysis, primarily class, are ignored. The overarching concepts are grounded in critical theory and a structural critique of education, yet race remains an elusive category.

This indicates that the study of race is embedded within a course but not necessarily a topic of required courses. Moreover, when multiculturalism and diversity are taught, they are often taught within a professional, as opposed to analytical, context. Professional courses focus on the methods, including inclusive classrooms "understanding learning, learner similarities and differences in diverse populations" (Syracuse, "Course Catalog, EDU 204," 2015). Another example from the institution is telling:

> Methods and materials to ensure that diverse student needs are met in classrooms. Focus on individual differences in learning, behavior, physical abilities, and emotional characteristics. Other differences will also be considered (e.g., race, gender). (Syracuse, "Course Catalog, SPE 412," 2015)

This instance is significant because it illustrates that race in this case is literally bracketed. The marginalization of race in the course description leaves the opportunity for discussion, but it certainly does not guarantee it.

These flagship programs illustrate that, in regard to the inclusion of race in the curriculum, diversity is the predominant topic. Education programs that promote diversity and related interests are more global in nature. In other words, race has boundaries. Conversely, diversity provides escape routes from dealing with issues of race. In examining the course titles, mission statements, and program descriptions, it appears that racial issues are given the opportunity to be addressed as part of a larger discussion about diversity. The fields of study examined have a great deal of depth, and the possible gains from exploring diversity should never be discounted, but does an in-depth examination of diversity get to the core of race? More importantly, do in-depth discussions about diversity reach the core of the future teacher who will inevitably have to deal with race?

RACE REVISITED AFTER THE TURN TOWARD DIVERSITY

Educators and our classrooms are called upon during this collective demand to root out racism in our institutional structures. Given the tragedies in Charleston, South Carolina, and Charlottesville, Virginia, and the national movement coalescing around the Black Lives Matter movement, which gained prominence in Ferguson, Missouri, many voices demand that educators revisit race in the classroom. This analysis revealed that teachers, for the most part, are prepared to meet the challenge with content in diversity and multiculturalism. The content and methodology of teacher education is strong, even setting national exemplars on how to approach the issue. Theories of race and humanity or social science–based examinations of race are evident, as noted, in the courses students are required to complete outside of teacher education programs. Moreover, institutional analyses reveal that students are exposed to (at least theoretically) critical theory or critical pedagogy, which is bolstered by strong content about race and racial formation in the humanities and social sciences. Yet aforementioned instances of harmful teaching in the classroom point toward a disconnect between teacher education programs and praxis that leads to harmful inclusions of race in the classroom.

Institutional imperfections mask the intentions of the programs to be more inclusive and "diverse." One such issue is how race is embedded within the larger discursive and analytic push toward diversity and multiculturalism. Diversity and multiculturalism assume we have "completed" race. Constructivism, a key tenet and foundation in teacher education programs, is built on scaffolding and on the notion that teacher educators can move on once a concept like race is mastered. Assuming this, it appears that teacher education programs have moved toward diversity without talking about race. Therefore, there is no guarantee that the topics of multiculturalism, diversity, or urban studies necessarily or extensively address issues of race.

Not only is race embedded or subsumed within the turn toward multiculturalism, it is one that has not gone uncontested (Ravitch, 1990). As Diane Ravitch suggests, inclusion or which viewpoints are to be included in the curriculum are volatile topics in debates that lead toward "political" discussions that distract both students and teachers from teaching and learning. The controversy stirred by a revision of AP history standards also demonstrates the contentious nature of "politicizing" the curriculum. The Republican National Committee issued a resolution that charged that the new curriculum "reflects a radically revisionist view of American history that emphasizes negative aspects of our nation's history while omitting or minimizing positive aspects" (Gerwertz, 2014, p. 1). History standards (long subject to criticism by both liberal and conservative pundits, think tanks, and scholars) demonstrate how controversial teaching of race or topics concerning race (such as placing more emphasis on race while downscaling an examination of the "founding fathers") outlines the perilous terrain of the social studies curriculum. Moreover, race-neutral language and the apparent preference for such neutral or "objective" analysis further reduces race to a problem. Popular and national discourse, in conjunction with a background in teacher education that privileges notions of multiculturalism or diversity, does much to hamper open and forthright discussions of race in our classroom.

The professional atmosphere is also discouraging to educators who seek to incorporate race in productive ways in the classroom. Hostile rumors, if not factual instances, are enough to discourage directly addressing the issue. Three teachers at Howard Middle School (a charter school in Washington, DC, that serves Howard University, a long-standing historically black college) were allegedly terminated for teaching about race (Demby, 2015). A teacher in Iowa was terminated after calling Mark Twain a racist (Flood, 2012). In Seattle, the issue took on more controversy when a teacher was removed from a school for teaching controversial issues of social justice. The teacher employed "courageous conversations," which dealt directly with race and gender. The district faulted the teacher for creating "a high degree of emotion for students or potential distress." Moreover, a statement released by the district that stated that race and social justice need to be taught, but to avoid placing "any child into a situation where he or she feels so intimidated by the manner in which these issues are being taught that the course is no longer effective" ("Popular Seattle Teacher Forced Out," 2013). To the casual observer and the vigilant educator, it can appear that educators are being penalized for including race in the curriculum. To further muddy popular perception, organizations as canonical as the NAACP have defended the moves of the districts to remove such teachers. This controversy begs the question: Just *how* do we teach about race?

A brief evaluation of existing "alternative" course material and programs proffers preliminary suggestions as to how teacher education programs, in conjunction with professional development offered by public school districts, can better prepare future educators to discuss issues of race in the social studies classroom. The program and curriculum that educators have suggested, such as the "Charleston Syllabus" (Williams, Williams, & Blain, 2016) or the material presented by the Zinn Education project, suggest potential directions professional development can take from the perspective of better equipping teachers to discuss race, culture, and diversity. These programs, where they exist, also include electives in high schools. Yet these opportunities are marginalized within the profession, and assuming such a distant position from the mainstream ensures that teaching about race remains just that: marginal. Simply put, the knowledge is there, but overarching discourse and public support are not. An integrative approach that fleshes out race and content simultaneously is needed, as the truth is, as we've unfortunately experienced, that healthy conversations about race for the betterment of all are needed every day. After acknowledging that stronger discussions of race are needed at *all* levels of teacher education, particularly professional development, these alternatives can be evaluated thoroughly.

Progressive forms of education must encourage progressive practices, especially when attending to racial groups that have been historically marginalized. Future teachers must learn to instruct their students to consider the possibilities of an equal and just multicultural society. For example, instead of having students play the traditional role of an oppressor or the oppressed in reenacting time, place, conditions, and situations, have them take the role of characters who are positioned to be the oppressor and the oppressed, analyze the related content, and create a play of the possibilities of being more than opportunistic and better than we were before. Instead of asking a student to bring a Klan hood into the classroom to share with classmates, prepare an in-depth lesson about the Klan, and instruct students to reflect and consider the purposes, fears, and feelings of power of the individuals whose faces were hidden behind the hood. Racial inequities of the past cannot be eradicated, but they can be explored within the constructs of progressive forms of education such as diversity and multicultural education. Teacher education programs are preparing teacher practitioners to understand the significance of creating a healthy classroom environment that embraces equality and fairness. As important, they must recognize the historically marginalized groups that are a part of the mosaic that makes diversity possible and attend to the historical context that creates unfortunate pitfalls in the K–12 classroom.

REFERENCES

Allen, A., Scott, L., & Lewis, C. W. (2013). Racial microaggressions and African American and Hispanic students in urban schools: A call for culturally affirming education. *Interdisciplinary Journal of Teaching & Learning, 3*(2), 117–29.

Anderson, M. (2018). What kids are really learning about slavery. *The Atlantic*. Retrieved from https://www.theatlantic.com/.../2018/...kids-are-really-learning-about-slavery/552098/.

Atwater, M., Butler, M. B., Freeman, T., & Carlton Parsons, E. (2013). An examination of black science teacher educators' experiences with multicultural education, equity, and social justice. *Journal of Science Teacher Education, 24*(8), 1230–1313.

Banks, J. (1995). Multicultural education and curriculum transformation. *Journal of Negro Education, 64*(4), 390–400.

Bennett, S. (2013). Effective facets of a field experience that contributed to eight preservice teachers' developing understandings about culturally responsive teaching. *Urban Education, 48*(3), 380–419.

Blum, L. (2012). *High schools, race, and America's future: What students can teach us about morality, diversity, and community*. Cambridge, MA: Harvard Education Press.

Bondy, E., Ross, D., Hambacher, E., & Acosta, M. (2012). Becoming warm demanders: Perspectives and practices of first-year teachers. *Urban Education, 48*(3), 420–50.

Brooks, J., & Brooks, M. (1999). *In Search of Understanding: The Case for Constructivist Classrooms.* Alexandria, VA: Association for Supervision and Curriculum Development.

Brown, E. (2007). The quiet disaster of No Child Left Behind: Standardization and deracialization breed inequality. In K. Saltman (Ed.), *Schooling and the politics of disaster* (pp. 123–40). New York, NY: Routledge.

Buehler, J., Gere, A. R., Dallavis, C., & Haviland, V. S. (2009). Normalizing the fraughtness: How emotion, race, and school context complicate cultural competence. *Journal of Teacher Education, 60*(4), 408–18.

Chapelfield Elementary School sorry for making black student "Slave." (2011, March 4). Retrieved from http://www.huffingtonpost.com/2011/03/04/chapelfield-elementary-sc_n_831318.html.

Civil rights movement education remains "woefully inadequate" in a majority of states. (2014). Southern Poverty Law Center. Retrieved from https://www.splcenter.org/news/2014/03/05/civil-rights-movement-education-remains-'woefully-inadequate'-majority-states-splc-report.

Darder, A. (2011). *A dissident voice: Essays on culture, pedagogy, and power.* New York, NY: Peter Lang.

Darling-Hammond, L. (2007). Race, inequality and educational accountability: The irony of No Child Left Behind. *Race, Ethnicity and Education, 10*(3), 245–60.

Delpit, L. (2006). *Other people's children: Cultural conflict in our classrooms.* New York, NY: W. W. Norton.

Demby, G. (2015, February 3). Lots of confusion over teacher firings at Howard University Middle School, *NPR, Code Switch.* Retrieved from http://www.npr.org/blogs/codeswitch/2013/07/24/205058168/.

Dewey, J. (1897). *My pedagogic creed. The School Journal, 54*(3), 77–80.

Dewey, J. (1916). *Democracy and education: An introduction to the philosophy of education.* New York, NY: Macmillan.

Dewey, J. (1938). *Experience and education.* New York, NY: Simon & Schuster.

Emdin, C. (2016). *For White folks who teach in the hood . . . and the rest of y'all too.* Boston, MA: Beacon Press.

Fallace, T. D. (2011). *Dewey and the dilemma of race: An intellectual history.* New York, NY: Teachers College Press.

Flood, A. (2012, July 18). *Teacher's aide sacked over claim that Huckleberry Finn is "racist."* Retrieved from http://www.theguardian.com/books/2012/jul/18/teacher-sacked-huckleberry-finn-racist.

Florida Atlantic University (FAU), Department of Curriculum, Culture, and Educational Inquiry (2015). Retrieved from https://www.fau.edu/education/academicdepartments/ccei/.

Florida Atlantic University (FAU), Master of Education in Curriculum. (2018). Retrieved from https://www.fau.edu/education/academicdepartments/ccei/mastersci/.

Florida Atlantic University (FAU), Education Specialist Degree in Curriculum and Instruction. (2018). Retrieved from https://www.fau.edu/education/academicdepartments/ccei/eds-curriculum-instruction/documents/eds-ci-program-description.pdf.

Florida Atlantic University (FAU), Master's Degree in Environmental Education. (2018). Retrieved from http://www.pinejog.fau.edu/student-programs/masters-degree.php.

Freire, P. (2002). *Pedagogy of the oppressed.* New York, NY: Continuum.

Fosnot, C. T. (Ed.). (1996). *Constructivism: Theory, perspectives, and practice.* New York, NY: Teachers College Press.

Gay, G. (2002). Preparing for culturally responsive teaching. *Journal of Teacher Education, 53*(2), 106–16.

Gay, G. (2013). Teaching to and through cultural diversity. *Curriculum Inquiry, 43*(1), 48–70.

Gerwertz, C. (2014, August 11). Republican National Committee condemns new AP history framework. *Education Week Blog.* Retrieved from http://blogs.edweek.org/edweek/curriculum/2014/08/college_board_statement_on_ap.html.

Gist, C. (2014). A Culturally responsive counter-narrative of effective teaching. *Cultural Studies of Science Education, 9*(4), 1009–14.

Gooden, M., & O'Doherty, A. (2015). Do you see what I see? Fostering aspiring leaders' racial awareness. *Urban Education, 50*(2), 380–419.

Griner, A. C., & Stewart, M. L. (2012). Addressing the achievement gap and disproportionality through the use of culturally responsive teaching practices. *Urban Education, 48*(4), 582–621.

Hachfeld, A., Hahn, A., Schroeder, S., Anders, Y., & Kunter, M. (2015). Should teachers be colorblind? How multicultural and egalitarian beliefs differentially relate to aspects of teachers' professional competence for teaching in diverse classrooms. *Teaching & Teacher Education, 48*, 44–55.

Harmon, D. A. (2012). Culturally responsive teaching through a historical lens: Will history repeat itself? *Interdisciplinary Journal of Teaching and Learning, 2*(1), 12–22.

Hawley, W., & Nieto, S. (2010). Another inconvenient truth: Race and ethnicity. *Educational Leadership, 68*(3), 66–71.

hooks, b. (1994). *Teaching to transgress: Education as the practice of freedom.* New York, NY: Routledge.

Jeffries, H., Blight, B., & Shuster, K. (2018). Teaching hard history: American slavery. Southern Poverty Law Center. Retrieved from https://www.tolerance.org/sites/default/files/2018-02/TT-Teaching-Hard-History-American-Slavery-Report-WEB-February2018.pdf.

Katrandjian, O. (2012, January 21). *Teacher who assigned math homework with slavery questions resigns.* Retrieved from http://abcnews.go.com/blogs/headlines/2012/01/teacher-who-assigned-math-homework-with-slavery-questions-resigns/.

KKK robes in class spark controversy in Las Vegas, teacher won't be punished. (2013, January 29). Retrieved from http://www.huffingtonpost.com/2013/01/29/kkk-robes-in-class-spark-_n_2574180.html.

Knaus, C. (2014). Seeing what they want to see: Racism and leadership development in urban schools. *Urban Review, 46*(3), 420–44.

Ladson-Billings, G. (2009). *The dream keepers: Successful teachers of African American children.* San Francisco, CA: John Wiley & Sons.

Lam, K. (2015). *Youth gangs, racism, and schooling: Vietnamese American youth in a postcolonial context.* New York, NY: Palgrave Macmillan.

Martell, C. (2013). Race and histories: Examining culturally relevant teaching in the U.S. history classroom. *Theory & Research in Social Education, 41*(1), 65–88.

Matias, C. E. (2013). Check yo' self before you wreck yo' self and our kids: Counterstories from culturally responsive White teachers? . . . to culturally responsive White teachers! *Journal of Teaching and Learning, 3*(2), 68–81.

Milner, H. R. (2008). Disrupting deficit notions of difference: Counter narratives of teachers and community in urban education. *Teaching and Teacher Education, 24*(6), 1573–98.

Milner, H. R. (2015). *Rac(e)ing to class: Confronting poverty and race in schools and classrooms.* Cambridge, MA: Harvard Education Press.

Ohio State University (OSU), Multicultural and Equity Studies in Education. (2015). Retrieved from https://ehe.osu.edu/teaching-and-learning/academics/multicultural-and-equity-studies-education.

Popular Seattle teacher forced out for teaching kids about racism. (2013). *Citizenship & Social Justice: Press Coverage*. Retrieved from http://citizenshipandsocialjustice.com/press/.

Ravitch, D. (1990). Multiculturalism: E Pluribus Plures. *The American Scholar, 59*(3), 337–54.

Sarraj, H., Bene, K., Li, J., & Burley, H. (2015). Raising cultural awareness of fifth grade students through multicultural education. *Multicultural Education, 22*(2), 39–45.

Shevalier, R., & McKenzie, B. A. (2012). Culturally responsive teaching as an ethics-and care-based approach to urban education. *Urban Education, 47*(6), 1086–1105.

Sleeter, C. (2012). Confronting the marginalization of culturally responsive pedagogy. *Urban Education, 47*(3), 562–84.

Syracuse University, School of Education. (2015). About the college. Retrieved from http://coursecatalog.syr.edu/content.php?catoid=3&navoid=256 .

Syracuse University, B.A. in Social Studies Education. (2015). Retrieved from http://soe.syr.edu/academic/undergraduate/social_studies_education/ .

Syracuse University, Cultural Foundations of Education. (2018). Faculty. Retrieved from http://soe.syr.edu/academic/cultural_foundations_of_education/faculty.aspx.

Syracuse University, Course Catalog, EDU 204, Principles of Learning in Inclusive Classrooms. (2015). Retrieved from http://coursecatalog.syr.edu/preview_course_nopop.php?catoid=3&coid=9931.

Syracuse University, Course Catalog, SPE 412, Adapting Instruction for Diverse Student Needs. (2015). Retrieved from http://coursecatalog.syr.edu/preview_course_nopop.php?catoid=3&coid=12834.

Theoharis, J. (2018). *A more beautiful and terrible history: The uses and misuses of civil rights history.* Boston, MA: Beacon Press.

Thomas, T. (2018). *Mother, student upset about slavery question in middle school class.* Gwinnet County, GA: WSB-TV.

Turner, C. (2018). Why schools fail to teach slavery's "hard history." *All things considered, National Public Radio.* Retrieved from https://www.npr.org/.../2018/.../why-schools-fail-to-teach-slaverys-hard-history

Ullucci, K., & Battey, D. (2011). Exposing color blindness/grounding color consciousness: Challenges for teacher education. *Urban Education, 46*(6), 1195–1225.

University of Georgia, College of Education. (2015). About the college. Retrieved from https://coe.uga.edu/about.

University of Georgia, College of Education (2015). Certificate in Diversity, Equity, and Inclusion. https://coe.uga.edu/academics/non-degree/certificate-diversity-equity-inclusion.

University of Nevada, Reno (UNV-R), College of Education. (2015). About Us/Mission. Retrieved from https://www.unr.edu/education/about-us.

University of Nevada, Reno (UNV-R), College of Education. (2015). University General Course Catalog. Retrieved from https://catalog.unr.edu.

University of Virginia, Curry School of Education. (2015). Syllabus for EDIS 5600, Teaching social studies in the secondary school. Retrieved from https://curry.virginia.edu/academics/social-studies-education.

University of Virginia, Curry School of Education. (2015). College of Arts & Sciences: Courses. Retrieved from http://records.ureg.virginia.edu/content.php?catoid=45&navoid=3203.

University of Virginia, Curry School of Education. (2018). Diversity at Curry. Retrieved from https://curry.virginia.edu/about-us/diversity-curry.

University of Virginia, Curry School of Education. (2018). Faculty & Staff. Retrieved from https://curry.virginia.edu/faculty-staff.

Valenzuela, A. (1999). *Subtractive schooling: U.S. Mexican youth and the politics of caring.* Albany, NY: State University of New York Press.

Vygotsky, L. S. (1978). *Mind in society: The development of higher psychological processes.* Cambridge, MA: Harvard University Press.

Walker, D. (2010, May 24). Catherine Ariemma, Georgia history teacher, let students wear Klan outfits. Retrieved from http://www.huffingtonpost.com/2010/05/24/catherine-ariemma-students-klan-outfits-video_n_588065.html.

Warren, C. (2013). The utility of empathy for white female teachers' culturally responsive interactions with black male students. *Interdisciplinary Journal of Teaching & Learning, 3*(3), 175–200.

Webley, K. (2011, April 12). Teacher puts black fourth graders "Up for Sale" in mock slave auction. Retrieved from http://newsfeed.time.com/2011/04/12/teacher-puts-black-fourth-graders-up-for-sale-in-mock-slave-auction/.

Whipp, J. (2013). Developing socially just teachers: The interaction of experiences before, during, and after teacher preparation in beginning urban teachers. *Journal of Teacher Education, 64*(5), 454–67.

Williams, C., Williams, K., & Blain, B. (2016). *Charleston syllabus: Readings on race, racism, and racial violence.* Athens, GA: University of Georgia Press.

Part Two

Dialogues of Teacher Education

In the chapters in the second half of this book, readers are invited join us in a venture to create a venue for giving voice to difficult problems of the day. Specifically, our purpose is to bring individuals together and engage in a meaningful, critical examination of selected topics that concern teacher educators and practitioners. We hope you enjoy the dialogue and that our contributing authors stimulate important and needed conversations among teacher educators, practitioners, policy makers, and other cultural workers concerned with improving teacher education and practice.

Chapter Five

Meeting the Challenge of Race and Poverty in Our Schools

The Role of Teacher Education

Patrick M. Jenlink

The theme of this dialogue draws into specific relief current discourses on how teacher education is preparing teachers for their role in contemporary society, hallmarked by issues of race and poverty impacting our schools and communities. Along this line, the theme is concerned with substantive treatment of identifying and exploring the priorities that recognized scholars believe to be of critical importance in advancing a new generation of teachers to address the issues of race and poverty and advancing the need for critical dialogues on race and poverty in teacher education and practice.

Poverty, race, segregation, and the current ideological trends in the United States emphasize the importance of changing the trajectory of teacher education to meet the challenge of ensuring that all children learn, regardless of racial/ethnic divides and the lack of emphasis on addressing poverty in our society. The critical concern for racialization of poverty, the intersectionality[1] of race/ethnicity, and the disturbing impact on schools and communities is a relevant point to consider in how we prepare teachers.[2] Another concern lies in preparing teachers for educational arenas in which they will interface with students who are socially and economically disadvantaged.

Addressing the economic disparity promoted through institutional racism is at the forefront of concerns that require attention. These will be priorities, among many, that are perceived as important to defining the work of teacher education in preparing teachers to confront the existing meta-narratives as they enter classrooms defined, in large part, by existing "cultural logic" and "social reality" that perpetuate the racial/ethnic divide and ignore the deep-seated problem of poverty. Munin (2012) makes an important point concerning poverty:

> Families of color are much more likely to live in poverty and thereby have less access to societal benefits granted to the economically privileged. However, it is important to point out that this [race and poverty] is not a perfect correlation. Not all people of color are poor, nor are all White people rich. It is very difficult to live in poverty, regardless of one's race. (p. 7)

What it means to live and learn each day without the necessary resources for success is at the root of this critical dialogue on race and poverty and the role of teacher education addressing the race/poverty concern in our schools and classrooms.

The reality of poverty and race is often difficult for teachers, in particular White teachers, to understand in relation to teaching non-White students of poverty and the difficulties those students face each day outside the classroom.[3] This is not to say that White students of poverty do not face similar difficulties; however, it does draw into specific relief a historical and endemic racial divide and how that divide often intersects with poverty.

Critical race theorists perceive issues of race and racism as permanent and endemic to the very fabric of society.[4] Issues of race/racism are endemic, woven deeply into the fabric of society, and race/racism will continue to be an area of importance in society and, consequently, education—even in mostly White social contexts or when discussions concern a majority of White people. Teacher education has a responsibility to immerse preservice teachers in dialogues on race/racism and the intersectionality of race and poverty.

Howard and Rodriquez-Scheel (2016) are instructive in stating a concern when considering the intersectionality of race and poverty and teacher preparation programs and whether the teacher educators in the program "have the willingness or the moral courage to engage in sensitive dialogues about poverty, race, gender, language, immigration, and other topics germane to marginalized groups" (p. 67). The authors posit a cautionary note with respect to the realization that as teacher educators, we have a responsibility to "not overlook the historical legacy of inequality that has been chronic for African

American, Latino, Native American, and certain Asian American groups" (p. 67).

The work of preparing teachers for their role in addressing racism and poverty requires teacher educators to engage preservice teachers in critical dialogues on race and poverty. Understanding and questioning, as Milner (2013) points out, "why a disproportionate number of students of color live in poverty and are from lower socioeconomic backgrounds" (p. 1) is a critical concern for preparing teachers to enter school classrooms where the reality of race and poverty will be experienced.

Teachers entering school classrooms for the first time, or in new and different geographies (rural, suburban, urban) should have an understanding of

> how systems of oppression, marginalization, racism, inequity, hegemony, and discrimination are pervasively present and ingrained in the fabric of policies, practices, institutions, and systems in education that have important bearings on students—all students—even though most of the studies reviewed did not address race in this way. (Milner, 2013, p. 1)

To not prepare teachers for the reality that students living in poverty face each day is to disadvantage the teachers and victimize the students even more than they already are, in the face of racism and poverty.

FINAL REFLECTIONS

There is a need for critical dialogue in preparing teachers for working with students in high-poverty schools because of the shifts that occur when it comes to structural versus individualistic ways of viewing the world. There is an equal need for critical dialogue in preparing teachers for working with the intersectionality of race and poverty and the complexity that emerges in lives of students and teachers and the larger community and society.

As teacher educators, if we could guide our preservice teachers to examine phenomena such as racism and life in poverty under a critical lens, coupled with a social justice frame, education could prove to be a powerful equalizer of the privileged and oppressed.

NOTES

1. McCall (2005) defines "intersectionality" as "the relationships among multiple dimensions and modalities of social relations and subject formations" (p. 1171). The complexity of intersectionality "arises when the subject of analysis expands to include multiple dimensions of social life and categories of analysis" (p. 1172). The intersectionality of race and poverty creates a level of complexity in conceptualizing discrimination and oppression within society.

2. Howard and Rodriquez-Scheel (2016) note that role of intersectionality in relation to teacher preparation: "The intersections of race, class, and gender have manifested in a multitude of complex and harmful ways within the U.S. that have profoundly influenced the manner in which students in low-income communities experience schools and society . . . therefore, it is essential that teacher-education programs incorporate readings, discussions, and films that require sustained focus on intersectionality and how it affects their teaching, as well as the students' identities as learners, and their academic outcomes" (p. 59).

3. Milner (2016) explains: "the most disturbing reality of living in poverty is the limitations of what low income and related resources allow people to do. For instance, it can be difficult for those in poverty to gain access to high-quality health care, to eat healthily especially fruits and vegetables that may be too expensive or that those living in poverty may have a difficult time acquiring due to the fact that they live in food deserts (often in rural spaces), or gain access and experience to high-quality, effective schools" (pp. 8–9).

4. See Crenshaw (2011), Crenshaw, Gotanda, Peller, & Thomas (1995), Delgado & Stefancic (2001), Ladson-Billings & Tate (1995), Ullucci (2012), Yosso (2005).

REFERENCES

Crenshaw, K. (2011). Twenty years of Critical Race Theory: Looking back to move forward. *Connecticut Law Review, 43*(5), 1253–1352.

Crenshaw, K. W., Gotanda, N., Peller, G. & Thomas, K. (1995). Introduction. In K. Crenshaw, N. Gotanda, G. Peller, & K. Thomas (Eds.), *Critical Race Theory: The Key Writings that Formed the Movement* (pp. xiii–xxii). New York, NY: New Press.

Delgado, R., & Stefancic, J. (2001). *Critical race theory: An introduction.* New York: New York University Press. Retrieved from: http://www.nyupress.org/19309chapt1.php.

Howard, T. C., & Rodriquez-Scheel, A. (2016). Difficult dialogues about race and poverty in teacher preparation. In J. Lampert & B. Burnett (Eds.), *Teacher education in high poverty schools* (pp. 53–72). Basel, Switzerland: Springer International.

Ladson-Billings, G., & Tate, W. F. (1995). Toward a critical race theory of education. *Teachers College Record, 97*, 47–68.

McCall, L. (2005). The complexity of intersectionality. *Journal of Women in Culture and Society, 30* (3), 1771–1800.

Milner, H. R. (2013). Analyzing poverty, learning, and teaching through a critical race theory lens. *Review of Research in Education, 37*, 1–53. DOI: 10.3102/0091732X12459720.

Munin, A. (2012). *Color by number: Understanding racism through facts and stats on children.* Sterling, VA: Stylus.

Ullucci, K. (2012). Learning to see: The development of race and class consciousness in White teachers. *Race, Ethnicity and Education, 14*, 561–77.

Yosso, T. J. (2005). Whose culture has capital? A critical race theory discussion of community cultural wealth. *Race, Ethnicity and Education, 8*(1), 69–91.

Chapter Six

What Do I Need to Know to Become a Teacher in Today's Schools?

Laveria F. Hutchison

Twenty-first-century learning skills, culturally responsive teaching, poverty, college and career-readiness concepts, choice and voice, students at risk, robotics technology, state assessments, demographics, and globalization are among the terms and concepts used today in educator preparation programs to explain the current K–12 educational landscape of the United States. As a teacher educator who wants to assist teacher candidates in learning to identify the skills needed to teach in today's schools, I believe an in-depth understanding of these terms and concepts is needed so that our teacher candidates will have the conceptual knowledge base needed to understand our educational system. As is historically known, student access to equal and fair educational systems has traditionally been a challenge for many racial and ethnic minorities in this country. This chapter uses a scenario and discussion of ideas for consideration in responding to the challenges often faced by teacher candidates who are preparing to become certified future educators.

SCENARIO

Roset is a senior at her university and a student teacher in an urban school. She was assigned as a student teacher in Ms. Fletcher's eighth-grade science class. Ms. Fletcher provides Roset with assessment data trends that reveal that the students in her class have a below-grade-level understanding of the science concepts and standards expected of middle-level eighth-grade students. As was suggested to her, Roset spends a significant amount of time reviewing the data and making notes to consider as she prepares to teach future lessons. While observing the students, Roset notices that a rather large number of them are reading below their grade level, are demonstrating a limited knowledge base of science concepts, are showing difficulty recording information, and are having challenges understanding English-delivered instruction. Roset's observations immediately prompt her to question *her readiness* to participate as a productive student teacher for the students in Ms. Fletcher's class by asking herself: Do I know how to teach literacy skills, do I have the knowledge to assess student learning, do I know how to use assessment data to plan and to deliver meaningful lessons, do I understand how to design instruction for English learners, and can I be successful in this instructional environment? Roset knows she has been an exceptional student who has received high grades in almost all of her science classes and methods classes in preparation for initial certification as a middle-level science teacher. In addition, she has read information and participated in group discussions about culturally responsive teaching practices. However, her initial thought from her observation of the landscape of Ms. Fletcher's class is that she may not be prepared to be successful as a student teacher.

DISCUSSION QUESTION

As the next generation of K–12 teachers, like Roset, are navigating the process of becoming certified to teach in a multicultural educational environment, what should their educator preparation programs include in the instruction, practice, and exposure of content so that K–12 students in classroom settings are receiving effective, culturally responsive, and engaging instruction that will be useful now as well as in the future?

Roset's scenario is not uncommon among student teachers who are becoming certified to provide instruction for K–12 students. As a teacher educator, I find Roset's situation to be of concern because her educator preparation program has provided her with limited knowledge and resources, which prevents her from feeling adequately prepared to serve as a student teacher who is also almost ready to become a certified and employed teacher. Roset and her peers needed early exposure to authentic classroom settings, lesson-planning experience, and lesson-delivery practice that would also allow for intentional critiques by her professors and peers and that would also provide a space for self-reflection. Her learning and implementation experiences should have addressed varied learning styles, increased skills in and knowledge of effective approaches for teaching English learners, along with instructional strategies that included literacy instruction and culturally responsive teaching strategies. Roset and her peers would also benefit from engaging in collaborative exchanges to discuss readings and media products and professional seminars that would cover a wide range of topics related to the current educational landscape of K–12 classrooms, the instructional needs of realistic academic environments, and the capacity to have opportunities to discuss and to implement research-based learning activities that would enhance the understanding of race, culture, identity, differentiated instructional practices, along with other concepts that would address the learning needs of students in school settings, along with learning effective ways to navigate the educational landscape of today's school settings.

Roset noticed the limited literacy of some of the students she observed. As she goes forward to become a certified teacher, she will need to be concerned about the reading levels and the command of print her students will need to develop through effective instruction and exposure to intentional practice. She will also need to teach her students to be critical thinkers, to adjust to the continuously changing requirements of digital literacy, and to have the capacity to solve problems that have not yet been identified. Educator preparation programs will need to assist their candidates in learning how to use accountability measures to aid in closing the achievement gap while understanding the nature of the opportunity gap that can exist among students in all types of school settings. As a teacher educator, I strongly believe that cultural exposure should go beyond the exterior consideration of family celebrations, food, and clothing to providing instructional information that considers the identities of K–12 students. Teacher candidates will need to acquire the capacity to implement pathways to provide opportunities for using resources to promote cultural exposure through educationally driven selected events while accepting their students' "funds of knowledge" through engagement with parents and community partners. Teacher educators should use varied instructional methods to expose their teacher candidates to multicultural literature and to diversity, both content and the delivery of pedagogical methods of instructional information, that will address the interest areas, background, and academic levels of K–12 students.

Trends have provided evidence of gains in educational access while still showing an achievement gap among racial- and ethnic-minority students (Lloyd, Tienda, & Zajacova, (2001; Current Population Surveys, 2013). College professors who teach in educator preparation programs should provide instruction and related resources that provide options to address academic standards that should be successfully met by students in K–12 school settings. Teacher educators should provide instruction that will assist teacher candidates in learning to diversify instructional options through delivered content, assessment practices, performance requirements, and learning strategies. Our teacher candidates will enter the teaching professional workforce facing a challenging educational landscape that is constantly changing. Education preparation programs will need to provide ways for their teacher candidates to understand the navigation of an educational system that is changing due to district, state, and national accountability requirements; students being expected to be college and career ready upon the completion of twelfth grade; student diversity; different learning styles and high-paced technological changes. In summary, educator preparation programs will need to equip teacher candidates with instructional opportunities that will allow for the continuation of responses to the challenges of our educational systems while providing evidence for our teacher candidates of the need to remain as academic learners by realizing and accepting the need to further their educational backgrounds through graduate-level education, attendance at professional education conferences, and attention to the academic needs and to the cultural identities of their K–12 students.

REFERENCES

Current Population Survey. (2013, April). *College enrollment and work activity of 2012 high school graduates* (Issue USDL-13-0670). Washington, DC: US Department of Labor, Bureau of Labor Statistics.

Lloyd, K. M., Tienda, M., & Zajacova, A. (2001). Trends in educational achievement of minority students since Brown v. Board of Education. In T. Ready, C. Edley, & C. Snow (Eds.), *Achieving high educational standards for all* (pp. 1–25). National Research Council. Washington, DC: National Academy Press.

Chapter Seven

High Expectations, Content, and Support

Carrie Robinson

I begin my reflection for this research monograph by acknowledging my belief that *all* parents, guardians, and caregivers send their most prized possessions, "their children," to America's schools to be educated. In addition, I believe that these parents, guardians, and caregivers expect that their children will be returned to them after schooling in far better shape academically than they were in when they entered the school system. The national pledge and charge to educate *all* children presents teacher educators with a plethora of both challenges and opportunities, given the rich tapestry of diversity and inclusion that make up the population in American society and schools. These challenges and opportunities can be used by teacher educators to promote a culture of evidence of a commitment to high expectations, high content, and high support as the foundation for academic excellence in classrooms, schools, school districts, and higher education institutions that prepare candidates for roles in schools.

The question: *What are the major responsibilities of educator preparers with respect to addressing race and poverty and therein implications for preparing the next generation of educators to meet the challenge?* is a controversial and timely topic/question in today's educational landscape in America. Based on my personal and professional experiences as a teacher educator in an urban institution of higher education, the question posed for the feature section of this book is very often the proverbial "elephant" in the room. By definition, teacher educators preparing candidates for myriad roles in schools that include, but are not limited to, teacher (preschool, elementary, middle, secondary, special education), counselor, educational leader, and supervisor send these aspiring educational candidates into different schools and school districts that *all* profess to provide an "equal educational opportunity" for learners. Additionally, the faculty and personnel in many, if not all or most, American schools and school districts assert that they believe that all children can learn *something.* This educational philosophy should provide the foundation for a commitment to high expectations in academic settings.

I believe that it is, therefore, unequivocally the responsibility of educator preparers to address issues of race and poverty in every program. The teacher educator's challenge to prepare candidates to morally and ethically address the challenges of race and poverty in America's schools is like politics. This daunting political challenge is local as well as simultaneously complex and simple. It is local because I do not believe that a single pedagogical approach exists that will adequately equip teacher educators in every higher education institution with the comprehensive knowledge base, skill set, and professional tools to prepare *all* candidates to effectively acknowledge, embrace, and appropriately address this question the same way in every school or school district.

The question is complex because while educator preparation institutions, colleges of education, departments, and programs may have in common some issues and challenges regarding the impact of race and poverty on education, no two urban, suburban, or rural schools or school districts are dealing with exactly the same nuances of the challenges associated with race and poverty in education. Therefore, I strongly recommend that teacher educators use the tenets of reality pedagogy as the raison d'être for program design, program implementation, and program evaluation to address these challenges and issues appropriately and comprehensively. In my preparation of aspiring school leaders, I embrace reality pedagogy because that approach to learning requires me to strive toward a professional practice that respects and values students as partners in the academic learning enterprise.

Cognizant of reality pedagogy, educator preparers must research and unpack the issues of race and poverty that are germane to the locale and milieu in which the educator preparation program exists and/or sends its candidates for clinical and internship experiences. I recommend that teacher educators use this research to frame their department's as well as their program's mission, vision, pedagogical content, professional and student standards, clinical experiences, and assessment plan. On this continuum of preparation, reality pedagogy should drive curriculum design. Curriculum implementation should drive the content of instruction. Pedagogical instruction should drive assessment. Assessment should drive curriculum design, curriculum implementation, and curriculum delivery to close the loop to address the challenges of race and poverty to meet the academic needs of specific learners in a local setting.

When student achievement data is disaggregated at the local level based on race, ethnicity, gender, and socioeconomic status, to name just a few significant variables, there is strong evidence that many children in these subgroups are not obtaining a quality education in their schools. This is not about blaming anyone but about how to best prepare educators to deal with this challenge in the local school and individual classroom to meet the academic needs of the individual learner. I do not subscribe to the deficit model often embraced by faculty and staff in many schools. I reject the simplicity of the achievement-gap label in favor of acknowledging that there is an opportunity gap and a digital divide in many schools. If school personnel value diversity and social justice, they do not lower their expectations of students based on race and/or socioeconomic status. Modeling the tenets of best professional practice, teacher educators should acknowledge that the background experiences of learners vary greatly. In addition, students enter schools and classrooms with very different academic and background experiences. They are met in the school setting by academic standards that vary and often lead to differences in curriculum content. Therefore, these variables should be taken into account by teacher educators in curriculum design, curriculum delivery/implementation, assessment of student learning, and evaluation of academic programs.

The pedagogical-program content that educator preparers must embrace to address the challenges of race and poverty in our schools should also be anchored in the research and contemporary best practices on cultural competence. In order to provide aspiring candidates (initial as well as advanced) with the knowledge, skills, and dispositions that will prepare them for a culture of practice in an educational setting that respects and values diversity and inclusion, teacher educators must strive for and demonstrate cultural competence in the higher education setting. Teacher educators as learners and facilitators of learning must model culturally competent behavior that builds intellectual capacity. To do this, teacher educators should first and foremost acknowledge that cultural, religious, gender, and sexual orientation are assets that should be used, valued, and respected in academic settings.

The goal of teacher education is to improve and enhance the academic mind set of all learners—aspiring teachers as well as P–12 learners. To accomplish this objective, I recommend that teacher educators employ three **HIGHS**—**HIGH** *expectations*, **HIGH** *content,* and **HIGH** *support*—to help aspiring educators address the challenge of race and poverty in education. I challenge teacher educators to demonstrate **high expectations** in their culturally proficient professional practice to prepare the next generation of learners by clearly articulating the appropriate learning objectives, standards, and methods of assessment that will be used for the specific learning population. When educators value and respect diversity (in all forms) and address issues of privilege and social justice in schools and schooling, they do not lower student standards/expectations based on race and/or conditions associated with poverty. I recommend that teacher educators demonstrate **high content** in their culturally proficient professional practice to prepare the next generation of learners by carefully and deliberately selecting diverse instructional materials for higher education and P–12 curricular content and experiences that reflect and value the diverse global village as a learning community that extends beyond the walls of the classroom. I recommend teacher educators demonstrate **high support** in their culturally proficient professional practice to prepare the next generation of aspiring educators to respect and value their student population as citizens of the global village. In order to provide **high support** for learners, teacher educators must recognize and work diligently to create a learning environment that creates rich academic opportunities for all learners and that simultaneously reconciles differences in the academic environment between and among cultures and subcultures. In addition, teacher educators should strive to avoid and eliminate stereotypes, prejudice, and privilege in their work to ensure that issues associated with race and poverty do not adversely affect the higher education learning community as well as P–12 students.

In conclusion, today's national discourse on teacher education is replete with competing ideas on how best to prepare the next generation of teachers. The role of teacher educators in meeting the challenges of race and poverty is a moral imperative and local initiative because faculty, staff, and education students must study their local communities and school populations. After identifying and studying issues of race and poverty in local communities, I recommend that teacher educators actualize academic excellence on school-by-school and student-by-student bases to embrace and advance the concept of high expectations, content, and support to fulfill the pledge of *equal educational opportunity* for all learners.

Chapter Eight

Teacher Educator Responsibilities for Preparing Teachers to Center Race

Adam Julian Alvarez

In 1968, the US Commission on Civil Rights (USCCR) conducted a case study of teachers in Syracuse, New York, following desegregation. The report explained that "teachers, mostly White, were frequently unprepared, indeed, reluctant, to deal with racial problems . . . lacked knowledge about racial problems and consequently were unable to cope with situations in desegregated classrooms" (p. 12). According to the USCCR report, only a voluntary workshop with no structured curriculum was in place to support teachers' understanding of race and race-related issues. Fifty years later, teachers today continue to express similar fears and feelings of unpreparedness related to in-class discussions about relevant issues related to race (Alvarez & Milner, in press), which could suggest that little has changed in terms of centering race in teacher education. Without opportunities to explore the centrality of race in teacher education programs, future teachers may not fully comprehend how race has been and continues to be a core feature of school and social inequality.

Before I introduce what I believe are three important teacher educator responsibilities for preparing teachers to center race, I want to suggest that much of the need for our focused instruction on addressing issues of race in schools and society stems from unjust institutional policies and practices. In fact, because institutions and systems have historically excluded people of color from economic and educational opportunities, numerous racial disparities persist inside and outside school. People of color, for instance, are more than twice as likely as White people to live at or below the poverty line (Proctor, Semega, & Kollar, 2016), which can dictate where families live and where their children can attend school. Compared to White children, children of color are more likely to live in areas with higher exposure to community violence (Fisher et al., 2018) and even harmful living conditions (Kozol, 2012). At the same time, such racial injustices have shaped the ways in which many White people, including teachers, think and talk about race and race-related issues (Milner, 2010).

CONVERGENCE, CONTEXT, AND CURRICULUM

It is critical to acknowledge that there is a need for what Milner (2008) called a disruptive movement in teacher education. Just as Milner has argued that individuals make systems, I believe that individual teacher educators can remake systems. Even if they do not have institutional support, individual teacher educators still have a responsibility to foreground issues of race and, ultimately, contribute to a broader shift toward centering race in the preparation of future teachers. I believe there is much we, as teacher educators, can do, but I want to focus on three responsibilities.

First, equity-focused teacher educators have a responsibility to converge with each other and develop synergistic relationships that center race. Coalitions of equity-focused teacher educators should involve a diverse group of people who discuss interdisciplinary research and teaching practices that recognize the centrality of race (Cochran-Smith, 1995). It is also paramount that coalitions of equity-focused teacher educators maintain a unified front, even in times of disagreement. To be clear, working toward a larger goal of equity means that teacher educators must be willing to remain critical but also compromise and support each other's efforts to enact structural change in teacher education programs and institutions more broadly.

Second, teacher educators have a responsibility to draw on macro- and micro- sociopolitical histories as they prepare future teachers to center race. Broadly, teacher educators must incorporate the influential role race has played in the United States, in terms of nation building and knowledge production. Exploring race from a contextual perspective should include dialogues related to power, privilege, and place. In a localized sense, teacher educators could benefit from building connections with community members and engaging in discussions about race and race-related issues (Alvarez, 2017). In particular, teacher educators can study the ways in which local communities and families make sense of broader sociopolitical issues related to race.

Third, teacher educators have a responsibility to design curricula that center race. If a teacher education curriculum can be seen as a plan for prioritizing knowledge teachers can access, a race-centered teacher education curriculum prioritizes racial knowledge. Race-centered curricula should incorporate time and discussion for teachers to reflect on their own racial identities. Teacher educators should also plan to encounter common tensions teachers have when issues of race emerge—from both historical and current events. Finally, using purposefully selected readings, interactive games, service-oriented group projects, and a host of others activities that can lead to generative dialogues about race, teacher educators can encourage a sense of activism and race engagement (Kokka, 2018).

FINAL THOUGHTS

Although much of what teachers learn prior to entering schools to teach falls on the institution, teacher educators, regardless of institutional support, have a responsibility to prepare teachers to center race in their practices. In particular, my contention is that teacher educators must a) converge to advance policies and practices that center race, b) draw on historical contexts to understand the influence of race, and c) design curricula that support future teachers' development of racial knowledge. We, as teacher educators, play a pivotal role in preparing future teachers to recognize and disrupt processes and systems that shape the lives and educational experiences of students of color. If we ignore our responsibilities to prepare future teachers to center race in their work, we can expect to be having a similar dialogue fifty years from now. More importantly, whether or not we take up our responsibilities as teacher educators could mean the difference in supporting or fighting against educational equity.

REFERENCES

Alvarez, A. J. (2017). "Seeing their eyes in the rearview mirror": Identifying and responding to students' challenging experiences. *Equity & Excellence in Education, 50*(1), 53–67.

Alvarez, A. J., & Milner, H. R. (in press). Race, violence, and teacher education: Exploring teachers' beliefs and feelings about race and police violence. *Teaching Education.*

Cochran-Smith, M. (1995). Uncertain allies: Understanding the boundaries of race and teaching. *Harvard Educational Review, 65*(4), 541–70.

Fisher, B. W., Viano, S., Curran, F. C., Pearman, F. A., & Gardella, J. H. (2018). Students' feelings of safety, exposure to violence and victimization, and authoritative school climate. *American Journal of Criminal Justice, 43*(1), 6–25.

Kokka, K. (2018). Radical STEM teacher activism: Collaborative organizing to sustain social justice pedagogy in STEM fields. *The Journal of Educational Foundations, 31*(1), 86–113.

Kozol, J. (2012). *Savage inequalities: Children in America's schools*. New York, NY: Broadway Books.

Milner, H. R. (2008). Critical race theory and interest convergence as analytic tools in teacher education policies and practices. *Journal of Teacher Education, 59*(4), 332–46.

Milner, H. R. (2010). *Start where you are, but don't stay there: Understanding diversity, opportunity gaps, and teaching in today's classrooms*. Cambridge, MA: Harvard Education Press.

Proctor, B. D., Semega, J. L., & Kollar, M. A. (2016). US census bureau, current population reports, P60-256 (RV), Income and poverty in the United States: 2015. Washington, DC: US Government Printing Office.

Chapter Nine

Real Talk about Race and Poverty

Danné E. Davis

Teacher educators must engage teacher candidates in *real talk* about their future work. A double entendre, real talk is an expression that opens or ends a statement of fact; in classrooms it describes honest, frank, sometimes messy conversations. The word *work* is intentional because effective teachers extend beyond scholastics. Teachers are social workers, health-care providers, even law enforcers! Educators must see the humanity of "other people's children" (Delpit, 2006) regardless of their last name or zip code. This appreciation is critical since the majority of public school teacher hopefuls are White women, with heteronormative views, from economically moderate households. In contrast, most Black and Brown K–12 learners are enrolled in underperforming public schools in cities with minimal or hard-to-access resources. This demographic divide signifies teacher candidates' superficial, enhanced-with-social-media-content understandings about kids and communities of color. This misperception contributes to the criminalization of Black and Brown boys, feeding the school-to-prison pipeline, restricting their behavior and self-determination, rather than cultivating brilliance and creativity. The adultification of Black girls is equally troubling.

Their calls to the profession are laced with the altruistic "save," "help the underprivileged," "give back" along with the commitment "never to see color." I respond with, "You don't have to be a teacher to do those things." Their reasons for wanting to teach echo Horace Mann's and W. E. B. Du-Bois's philosophical beliefs of education as the great equalizer. However, under attack is the supposition that a well-educated person will acquire the requisite knowledge, skills, and social capital to productively navigate our world. The impact of race and poverty fuels the attack. As teacher educators, our work includes engaging teacher hopefuls in *real talk* to facilitate rearranging their impassioned goals with truths about race and poverty when teaching in twenty-first-century public schools.

REAL TALK #1: I'M BLACK AND I'M PROUD!

Colorblindness is not an option. African American youth are confronted daily by blackness. Black pupil populations have an increasing presence in US public schools. In 2014, US public schools reached a "majority-minority milestone," which, according to census watchers, acknowledged that children of color collectively surpassed White K–12 public school enrollment. Whether by design or happenstance, ignoring the race, ethnicity, and cultural identity of students of color says to them, "You are not important." Teachers who fail to see color dismiss the lived experience and contributions of an entire people. Colorblindness denies all learners from gaining awareness of and respect for the global community. This dismissal is akin to cultural elimination—the intentional subtraction of a segment of humanity; an entire group of people made insignificant. Colorblindness is not acceptable. Rather, it is today's "new racism."

Whether it's called "multicultural education," "antiracist praxis," "culturally responsive/relevant" teaching or pedagogy, teacher educators must ensure that teacher candidates recognize, then use, the lived experiences of *every* child, especially Black and Brown youth. The existence, significance, and contributions of students' ancestors require inclusion in the curriculum. Real talk about those histories—but more importantly dissecting the practices and motives that discount those narratives, inside and outside school—adds color to the teacher education curriculum.

REAL TALK #2: FULL OF FUNDS . . . OF KNOWLEDGE

During each of my first class introductions, I show a PowerPoint slide with a picture of my childhood home. Routinely, I hear "oohs and ahhs" from the teacher hopefuls when they see the red, two-story, eleven-room Victorian house, positioned on a Boston—that is, big city/urban—tree-lined street. When the reactions cease, I share details of my lived experiences with immediate and extended family; about schooling and community. My family was not wealthy. Rather, everything that I had, saw, and encountered was the result of a hardworking father and determined mother. They took advantage of every free community resource and church event—all of which we accessed to enhance my worldview for full adult participation when the time arrived.

It is critical for teacher candidates to recognize that big-city/urban living does not equate to deficiency and depravity. From a public housing unit to a private family dwelling similar to mine in Boston, each household contains "funds of knowledge" (González, Moll, & Amanti, 2009)—unique skills, understandings, and know-hows acquired through myriad family-member interactions. Of note is the concept of family—a group of loving human beings with shared DNA who function as a unit. Particularly, for many Black people, extended relatives and other persons without common biology tend to view themselves as family. Students' homes are a treasure trove of useful resources. Those resources comprise family traditions, milestones, innovation, and more. Teacher educators must position teacher candidates to appreciate the value of students' home life by accessing their funds of knowledge.

REAL TALK #3: NO, I'D RATHER NOT SMILE

From yellow stickers to the happy classroom bear, smiles are prevalent, especially in elementary schools. However, extant research confirms that poor dental health affects school attendance, academic performance, and psychological well-being. Regarding attendance, toothaches, oral pain, and dental problems are major pilferers. Children who attend school with dental discomfort are easily bored and unengaged because of the pain. A sustained disconnect creates apathy that impedes scholastic growth. Whatever the cause, when students feel bad or look bad—as often happens with oral/dental disease—no amount of school "fun" is going to spur engagement. Field experiences with dental health professionals invite opportunities to discover best practice pediatric dental care and also grasp troubleshooting measures. Other health problems resulting from impoverished situations include: (a) misery and uncertainty; (b) low food security, meaning reduced quality, choice, and meal attraction, or very low food security, whereby children experience multiple eating interruptions and reduction of food intake; and (c) changes to the brain that reduce cognition. However, poverty and its residuals must be deemed opportunity gaps.

Race and poverty continue to impact life in US schools. I remain committed to engaging in real talk about the harms of colorblindness, the importance of teaching in ways that value everyone, and caring for the "the village." Are you ready to join me?

REFERENCES

Delpit, L. (2006). *Other people's children: Cultural conflict in the classroom.* New York, NY: The New Press.

González, N., Moll, L. C., & Amanti, C. (2009). *Funds of knowledge: Theorizing practices in households, communities, and classrooms.* New York, NY: Routledge.

Chapter Ten

Adopting a Complex, Decentered Perspective of Teaching Marginalized Students

Kathryn Strom

There is a large body of literature spanning three decades that addresses the preparation of teachers for culturally and linguistically diverse populations (e.g., Gay, 2000; Ladson-Billings, 1995; Lucas & Villegas, 2013; Paris & Alim, 2017). Generally this literature agrees that teachers of students whose demographics differ from the dominant culture (e.g., White, middle-class or affluent, English speaking, Christian) should develop assets-based perspectives, understand sociopolitical contexts of education, and teach from a sociocultural pedagogical perspective that grounds curriculum in student knowledge and resources (Lucas & Villegas, 2013; Paris & Alim, 2017; Villegas & Lucas, 2002). However, despite consensus among many well-respected scholars of teacher education regarding what needs to be done pedagogically to support historically marginalized and minoritized student populations, translating that knowledge into classroom practice remains a challenge for teachers (Chubbuck, 2008; McDonough, 2009; Strom, 2015). I argue that we need to reexamine the disconnect between what teachers learn about how to teach diverse, high-poverty populations and what actually happens in classrooms from a philosophical standpoint. Specifically, I argue that teacher educators need to make an *onto-epistemological shift* in thinking (Barad, 2007)—one that moves away from the individualistic, linear, reductionist logic of rational humanism and instead emphasizes a complex, multifaceted, interactional, interconnected, contextual, mobile, difference-rich worldview

(Strom & Martin, 2017). This shift, in turn, needs to inform how we prepare teachers for increasingly complex and politicized school contexts.

The work of the teacher is not something done by an autonomous actor as a one-way transaction—it is, rather, the joint production of an assemblage or multiplicity that includes, at a minimum, the teacher, her students, and contextual elements (e.g., class size, testing policies, school culture, supports and resources available, and so on) (Strom, 2015). The transmission view of teaching, as well as the current neoliberal "era of accountability" that grades teachers and students via standardized test scores, perpetuates the idea that teachers and students are individuals with complete agency (whether over teaching or learning) and, as such, unencumbered by things like historical conditions, available resources, or events that occur in lives outside of school. This idea of the a-contextual individual directly contradicts current understandings of learning upon which culturally and linguistically responsive pedagogy rest (Lucas & Villegas, 2013; Villegas & Lucas, 2002)—that is, that learning occurs socially, in collaborative and participatory environments, and must be grounded in students' academic, linguistic, and/or cultural knowledge. To better prepare teachers to teach in ways that result in powerful learning for marginalized students means that they need to shift away from individualistic views of teaching and learning and instead see themselves as part of a larger teacher-learner multiplicity.

Beyond pedagogical contradictions, the notion of the agentic, bounded individual is also one that underscores ideas like "grit" (a modern iteration of the "bootstraps" narrative), deficit thinking, and the notion of the "achievement gap"—all of which are harmful to students of color and other marginalized populations. By locating "problems" within the individual student her- or himself, and assuming they have total agency, we construct narratives that say they can "overcome" these problems with individual effort, or "grit." When they ultimately cannot grit their teeth and overcome White supremacy singlehandedly, deficit thinking is perpetuated. That is, educators can continue to blame the student rather than examining the system within which the student resides and the way power operates within it (including the ways that the teacher herself is plugged into that system/power). The language and reforms of the "achievement gap" also reinforce the notion that the students contain the deficit—rather than helping teachers understand, as Ladson-Billings (2006) has argued, that this "gap" is actually a debt owed students of color from over a century of systemic educational oppression.

Teacher educators, then, have a responsibility to help teachers develop a decentered view of themselves, their students, and their teaching: to understand that teaching is a heavily mediated act, that teachers are only partially agentic, and that they—and their students—are embedded in webs of systems of power and historical conditions that also play a role both in the ways they teach and the educational access afforded their marginalized students. As one way of taking into account the collective nature of teaching, teacher educators can make the interactive, negotiational aspect of instruction a centerpiece of initial teacher preparation in field settings or through "approximations" of practice (Grossman et al., 2009). Learning opportunities that highlight the heavily mediated nature of teaching will help teachers appreciate shared agency and disrupt notions of the autonomous individual, which can help them develop a more coherent ontological perspective more aligned with the sociocultural theoretical basis of culturally and linguistically responsive pedagogy. Further, teachers can engage in critical reflection and dialogue to locate and account for themselves in relation to their students, pedagogy, and curriculum. This, in turn, helps future teachers develop a view of themselves, and their students, as connected to, and in fact inextricable from, certain histories, material conditions, and systems of power that perpetuate conditions of inequality. From this point of understanding, teachers can examine their beliefs, instructional practices, and interactions with students and analyze how those might be working to perpetuate or disrupt the continued operation of systems of oppression in schools.

REFERENCES

Barad, K. (2007). *Meeting the universe halfway: Quantum physics and the entanglement of matter and meaning.* Durham, NC: Duke University Press.

Chubbuck, S. M. (2008). A novice teacher's beliefs about socially just teaching: Dialogue of many voices. *The New Educator, 4*(4), 309–29.

Gay, G. (2000). *Culturally responsive teaching: Theory, practice and research.* New York, NY: Teachers College Press.

Grossman, P., Compton, C., Igra, D., Ronfeldt, M., Shahan, E., & Williamson, P. (2009). Teaching practice: A cross-professional perspective. *Teachers College Record, 111*(9), 2055–2100.

Ladson-Billings, G. (1995). Toward a theory of culturally relevant pedagogy. *American Educational Research Journal, 32*(3), 465–91.

Ladson-Billings, G. (2006). From the achievement gap to the education debt: Understanding achievement in US schools. *Educational researcher, 35*(7), 3–12.

Lucas, T., & Villegas, A. M. (2013). Preparing linguistically responsive teachers: Laying the foundation in preservice teacher education. *Theory into Practice, 52*(2), 98–109.

McDonough, K. (2009). Pathways to critical consciousness: A first-year teacher's engagement with issues of race and equity. *Journal of Teacher Education, 60*(5), 528–37.

Paris, D., & Alim, H. S. (Eds.). (2017). *Culturally sustaining pedagogies: Teaching and learning for justice in a changing world*. New York, NY: Teachers College Press.

Strom, K. J. (2015). Teaching as assemblage: Negotiating learning and practice in the first year of teaching. *Journal of Teacher Education, 66*(4), 321–33.

Strom, K. J., & Martin, A. D. (2017). *Becoming-teacher: A rhizomatic look at first-year teaching*. Dordrecht: Springer.

Villegas, A. M., & Lucas, T. (2002). Preparing culturally responsive teachers: Rethinking the curriculum. *Journal of Teacher Education, 53*(1), 20–32.

Chapter Eleven

Toward a Critical Race Theory for Teacher Education

Daniel G. Solorzano

I have been asked to respond this question: What are the major responsibilities of teacher educators with respect to addressing race and poverty and therein the implications for preparing the next generations of teachers to meet the challenges before us? I will begin by telling my story of how I continue to deal with questions that center race and racism at their intersections with other forms of marginality such as class and poverty. I will conclude by sharing a direction for teacher education using critical race theory in teacher education (CRTTE).

I begin by defining race and racism. Race, I argue, is a socially constructed category used to differentiate and justify the superiority or dominance of one race (i.e., whites) over others (i.e., People of Color). Racism is the belief in the inherent superiority of one race (i.e., whites) over others (i.e., People of Color) in order to justify unequal social arrangements and is tied to institutional power to enact those unjust social arrangements.

Critical race theory (CRT) in the law emerged in the mid-1980s from the work of legal scholars, lawyers, and activists (see Bell, 1992; Crenshaw et al., 1995; Delgado & Stefancic, 2017; Matsuda et al., 1993). This new framework challenged the dominant discourse on race and racism by examining how legal doctrine and practice were used to subordinate and marginalize certain racial and ethnic groups. In the mid-1990s, CRT moved to the field of education (see Ladson-Billings & Tate, 1995; Solorzano, 1997; Tate, 1994). Expanding on CRT legal scholarship and incorporating some of the transformative work in Chicana/o, African American, Native American, and Asian American studies, I argue that CRTTE is the work of scholars and practitioners who are attempting to develop an explanatory framework that accounts for the role of race and racism in teacher education and that works toward identifying and challenging racism as part of a larger goal of recognizing and disrupting all forms of subordination in schools and other social institutions (see Solorzano, 1997; 1998). With this definition in hand, I have developed, adapted, and applied five tenets for a CRTTE (see Solorzano, 1997):

Tenet 1. CRTTE foregrounds race and racism and challenges separate discourses on race, gender, and class by demonstrating how racism intersects with other forms of subordination (i.e., sexism, classism, Eurocentrism, monolingualism, and heterosexism) and how they impact Students of Color. *Application:* As we prepare teachers, we need to center our conversations on racism in both its interpersonal and institutional forms and how racism intersects with other forms of marginalization (i.e., classism and poverty). We need to ask the race and racism questions in our development and application of curriculum and pedagogy.

Tenet 2. CRTTE challenges traditional research paradigms and theories, thereby exposing deficit notions about Students of Color and educational policies and practices that assume "neutrality," "meritocracy," and "objectivity." *Application:* Deficit frameworks have been embedded in the way we train teachers for well over a century. We must challenge cultural-deficit frameworks that have been embedded in social science research for at least a century (see Romano, 1968). The tradition of explicit antideficit and antiracist frameworks has been part of social science and teacher educational research for close to seventy years. Although not exhaustive, these frameworks and educational movements in teacher education include bilingual education, bicultural education, multicultural education, Freirean education, critical pedagogy, effective schools, funds of knowledge, and community cultural wealth (see Sleeter & Delgado Bernal, 2004; Solorzano & Solorzano, 1995).

Tenet 3. CRTTE focuses research, curriculum, pedagogy, and practice on the lived experiences of Students of Color and regards these experiences as assets and sources of strength. *Application:* As we challenge deficit and racist frameworks, we must use antideficit and antiracist strength- and asset-based frameworks. Although not exhaustive, these can include culturally responsive and sustaining curriculum and pedagogy (see Howard, 2010; Ladson-Billings, 1995; Paris, 2012), funds of knowledge (see Moll et al., 1992), and community cultural wealth (see Yosso, 2005; Yosso & Solorzano, 2005).

Tenet 4. CRTTE offers a transformative solution to racial, gender, and class discrimination by linking theory with practice, scholarship with teaching, and the academy with the community. *Application:* As we prepare teachers to serve Communities of Color, we must provide social justice tools for our teachers and their students. In the Freirean tradition, CRTTE names racist injuries (i.e., names the problem), identifies their origins (i.e., analyzes the causes), and seeks remedies for the injury (i.e., finds solutions) (see Freire, 1970; 1973).

Tenet 5. CRTTE challenges ahistoricism and acontextualism, and insists on expanding the boundaries of the analysis of race and racism in education by using contextual, historical, and interdisciplinary perspectives to inform praxis. *Application:* The fields of race and ethnic studies and gender and women's studies have and will continue to provide tools for our teachers and their students to identify, analyze, and take action against interpersonal and institutional forms of marginalization. As we prepare our teachers for the classroom, we must remember that the challenges they and their students encounter in and out of the classroom have historical and contextual roots and that history and context can provide guidance to meeting those challenges.

Most of the social science research asserts that US educational institutions marginalize the experiences and histories of People of Color. Educational marginalization is often justified through research and teaching that decenters and indeed dismisses the histories and experiences of Communities of Color. Teacher educators and their students should continually ask "Whose stories are privileged in educational contexts and whose stories are distorted and silenced?" US history reveals that white upper- and middle-class stories are privileged, whereas the stories of People of Color are distorted and silenced. We should further ask "What are the experiences and responses of those whose stories are often distorted and silenced?" Teacher educators and their students should be in the forefront in documenting the voices and stories of People of Color.

CRTTE offers a way to honor and understand the experiences of People of Color along the educational pipeline. Such theory and practice generate knowledge by looking to those who have been marginalized, silenced, and disempowered. CRTTE challenges traditional theories, methodologies, and pedagogies because it requires us to use other theories of social transformation (i.e., Black feminist theories, Chicana feminist theories, Women of Color feminisms). CRTTE focuses research on how Students of Color experience and respond to an educational system—a system that devalues and dehumanizes them. From developing research questions to collecting, analyzing, and presenting data, CRTTE centers on the lives and experiences of Students of Color. Using CRTTE confirms that we must look to how Students of Color respond to everyday racism, sexism, classism, and heterosexism in and out of schools. CRTTE contextualizes Student-of-Color experiences in the past, present, and future. It strategically uses multiple methods, often unconventional and creative, to draw on the knowledge of People of Color, who are traditionally excluded from being an official part of the academy and the schools. CRTTE challenges deficiency stories through counter-storytelling, oral traditions, life histories, folk tales, poetry, films, theater, music, humor, or other means.

CRTTE also argues that what is noticeably missing from the discussion of race is a substantive discussion of racism in teacher education. I believe CRTTE can move us forward in these discussions. As we work with and for those at the margins of society, we hold on to the belief that the margin can be "more than a site of deprivation . . . it is also the site of radical possibility, a space of resistance" (hooks, 1990, p. 149). Anzaldúa (1990) explains:

> Theory, then, is a set of knowledges. Some of these knowledges have been kept from us—entry into some professions and academia denied us. Because we are not allowed to enter discourse, because we are often disqualified and excluded from it, because what passes for theory these days is forbidden territory for us, it is vital that we occupy theorizing space, that we not allow white men and women solely to occupy it. By bringing in our own approaches and methodologies, we transform that theorizing space. (p. xxv)

We argue that CRTTE, with its counterstories and even poetic modes of expression (Solorzano, 1997; Solorzano & Yosso, 2001), articulates a response to Anzaldúa's (1990) challenge that "if we have been gagged and disempowered by theories, we can also be loosened and empowered by theories" (p. xxvi). Our response draws on the strengths of Communities of Color. If theories and methodologies have been used to silence and marginalize People of Color, then theories and methodologies can also give voice and turn the margins into places of transformative resistance (Solorzano & Delgado Bernal, 2001). We know that many would discount the histories, experiences, and lives of People of Color. Revealing the deficit discourse in majoritarian stories reveals white privilege, and this often is perceived as a threat to those who benefit from racism. However, as a strategy of survival and a means of resistance, CRTTE will continue to work to tell the counter-stories of those "at the bottom of society's well" (Bell, 1992, p. v).

This CRTTE framework is one way I come to answer the question posed: What are the major responsibilities of teacher educators with respect to addressing race and poverty and therein the implications for preparing the next generations of teachers to meet the challenges before us?

REFERENCES

Anzaldúa, G. (1990). *Haciendo caras, una entrada*. In G. Anzaldúa (Ed.), *Making face, making soul: Creative and critical perspectives by Feminists of Color* (pp. xv–xxviii). San Francisco, CA: Aunt Lute Books.

Bell, D. (1992). *Faces at the bottom of the well: The permanence of racism*. New York, NY: Basic Books.

Crenshaw, K., Gotanda, N., Peller, G., & Thomas, K. (Eds.). (1995). *Critical race theory: The key writings that formed the movement*. New York, NY: The New Press.

Delgado, R., & Stefancic, J. (2017). *Critical race theory: An introduction* (3rd ed.). New York, NY: New York University Press.

Freire, P. (1970). *Cultural action for freedom*. Cambridge, MA: Harvard Educational Review Monograph.

Freire, P. (1973). *Pedagogy of the oppressed*. New York, NY: Seabury Press.

hooks, b. (1990). *Yearning: Race, gender, and cultural politics*. Boston, MA: South End Press.

Howard, T. (2010). *Why race and culture matter in schools: Closing the achievement gap in America's classrooms*. New York, NY: Teachers College Press.

Ladson-Billings, G. (1995). Toward a theory of culturally relevant pedagogy. *American Educational Research Journal, 32*, 465–91.

Ladson-Billings, G., & Tate, W. (1995). Toward a critical race theory of education. *Teachers College Record, 97*, 47–68.

Matsuda, M., Lawrence, C., Delgado, R., & Crenshaw, K. (1993). *Words that wound: Critical race theory, assaultive speech, and the first amendment*. Boulder, CO: Westview Press.

Moll, L. C., Amanti, C., Neff, D., & Gonzalez, N. (1992) Funds of knowledge for teaching: Using a qualitative approach to connect homes and classrooms. *Theory into Practice, 31*, 132–41.

Paris, D. (2012). Culturally sustaining pedagogy: A needed change in stance, terminology, and practice. *Educational Researcher, 41*, 93–97.

Romano, O. (1968). The anthropology and sociology of the Mexican American. *El Grito: The Journal of Contemporary Mexican-American Thought, 2*, 13–26.

Sleeter, C., & Delgado Bernal, D. (2004). Critical pedagogy, critical race theory, and antiracist education: Implications for multicultural education. In J. Banks & C. Magee Banks (Eds.), *Handbook of research on multicultural education* (2nd ed.) (pp. 240–57). San Francisco, CA: Jossey Bass.

Solorzano, D. (1997). Images and words that wound: Critical race theory, racial stereotyping, and teacher education. *Teacher Education Quarterly, 24*, 5–19.

Solorzano, D. (1998). Critical race theory, race and gender microaggressions, and the experience of Chicana and Chicano scholars. *International Journal of Qualitative Studies in Education, 11*, 121–36.

Solorzano, D., & Bernal, D. D. (2001). Examining transformational resistance through a critical race and LatCrit theory framework: Chicana and Chicano students in an urban context. *Urban Education, 36*, 308–42.

Solorzano, D., & Solorzano, R. (1995). The Chicano educational experience: A proposed framework for effective schools in Chicano communities. *Educational Policy, 9*, 293–314.

Solorzano, D., & Yosso, T. (2001). Critical race and LatCrit theory and method: Counterstory-telling. *International Journal of Qualitative Studies in Education, 14*, 471–95.

Tate, W. (1994). From inner city to ivory tower: Does my voice matter in the academy? *Urban Education, 29*, 245–69.

Yosso, T. (2005). Whose culture has capital? A critical race theory discussion of community cultural wealth. *Race Ethnicity and Education, 8*, 69–91.

Yosso, T. & Solorzano, D. (2005). Conceptualizing a critical race theory in sociology. In M. Romero and E. Margolis (Eds.), *Blackwell companion to social inequalities* (pp. 117–46). London, UK: Blackwell.

Chapter Twelve

Reimagining Three Responsibilities of Teacher Education/Preparation

Structural Racism, Poverty, and Implicit Bias

Sherick Hughes and Ronda Taylor Bullock

Irrespective of the type, length, and location of their programs, teacher educators play a pivotal role in preparing the next generations of teachers. Therefore, they have responsibilities to address the influence of race and poverty, which often function as systemic social barriers to teaching and learning (Hughes & Berry, 2012). Life expectancy, educational outcomes, and access to health care are all dictated disproportionately by biased reactions to race and socioeconomic status (Payne, Niemi, & Doris, 2018). Students and teachers do not leave social labels behind when they enter classrooms (Warikoo et al., 2016). It is imperative that teacher educators gain a structural understanding of race and class. In doing so, they will see how racism and poverty are historically connected to the educational system daily (Hughes & Berry, 2012). This chapter responds to the following question: What are the major responsibilities of teacher educators with respect to addressing race and poverty and therein the implications for preparing the next generations of teachers to meet the challenges before us? Ultimately, we draw from current peer-reviewed research to: (a) propose a reimagining of three major responsibilities for teacher education/preparation programs with respect to understanding racism, poverty, implicit bias, and antibias and (b) offer some implications of this proposal for preparing future teachers.

REIMAGINING RESPONSIBILITIES OF TEACHER EDUCATION/ PREPARATION PROGRAMS

Responsibility 1: Emphasizing Structural Racism and Poverty

A major responsibility emerging from the literature for teacher education/ preparation programs to reimagine involves helping preservice teachers shift from thinking about race, per se, to thinking about race in relation to the historical, endemic nature of structural racism and its inextricable link to poverty (Hughes & Berry, 2012). This shift requires teachers to learn how to contextualize the systematic impact of racism and poverty. Some teacher education/preparation programs have made steps toward helping educators think about student achievement disaggregated by race (some still lag in this area). Others have also made steps toward incorporating culturally sustaining pedagogy and student cultures into the curriculum (Hughes & Berry, 2012). Consequently, a missing next step for those programs to consider is helping future teachers understand structural racism and poverty and their connection to education.

A historical, structural analysis of racism and poverty is imagined as another new normal in teacher education/preparation programs that could help teachers better understand present realities, not only in our field, but also in our society as a whole. For example, teachers' understandings of current educational plights of local Black, Latino, Indigenous, and impoverished families could be influenced by knowing that race as experienced in the United States today was reinforced by White-male property owners in the 1600s who reengineered race as a social construct to keep working-class Whites poor and Blacks in bondage and to prevent the two groups from joining forces (Hughes & Berry, 2012). Access to education is intertwined with racism and poverty—from segregation to disproportionate access to academically gifted classes to suspension rates (Warikoo et al., 2016). Having a systemic analysis as part of teacher education/preparation programs could empower teachers with the tools to make connections across, and to challenge, multiple racialized and classed systems that can influence teaching and learning.

Responsibility 2: Owning Teacher Bias

Recent research on implicit association bias in education also provides evidence to support teacher education/preparation programs' reimagining their responsibilities for helping pre-service teachers engage in critical self-aware-ness by understanding and owning their biases (Warikoo et al., 2016). The mandatory implementation of training toward recognizing and challenging implicit biases could be at the forefront of fulfilling these responsibilities. Implicit biases set people up to overgeneralize about a person or group of people that exists on a subconscious level, sometimes leading to discrimina-tion even when people feel they are being fair (Payne, Niemi, & Doris, 2018). They represent our blind spots. One narrative example that has be-come quite common features a teacher who may not recognize that all of the books she reads to her culturally and economically diverse class feature white middle- and wealthy-class, male-protagonist characters. A study by Kumar, Karabenick, and Burgoon (2015) found teachers with pro-White/ anti-Arab implicit associations to be less likely to try leading and sustaining a culturally sustaining classroom environment and less likely to facilitate reso-lutions when interethnic conflicts emerged in the classroom. Indeed, we all carry biases, regardless of our racial or ethnic background. A 2010 study found Dutch elementary school teachers' pro–native Dutch/anti-Turkish-Mo-roccan implicit association biases "were associated with lower expectations of their Turkish and Moroccan students, which in turn predicted lower aca-demic performance for these students" (Warikoo et al., 2016, p. 510). These biases carry systemic weight, particularly for kids of color.

Teacher biases can influence the ways in which students of color are disciplined (Skiba et al., 2011). In another common example, we often learn of teachers who may not be cognizant that she or he inequitably writes up Black and Latino males for disruptive behavior and only refers Black, Lati-no, and impoverished males (including impoverished White males) for spe-cial education as a result of such behavior. Discipline practices are connected to maintaining the school-to-prison pipeline, where students who are sus-pended from school are more likely to end up in prison. Scholars Okonofua and Eberhardt (2015) report that teachers more harshly punish students they perceive as Black, based solely on their names. While everyone, regardless of racial or ethnic identity, carries biases, roughly 80 percent of America's teachers are White (Loewus, 2017), while a majority of public schools are filled with students of color, whose percentage is growing (NCES, 2015).

If White teachers are like other adults, we can expect that "a majority hold medium to large negative associations about Black children and adults" (Warikoo et al., 2016, p. 509). There is robust data to support this expectation from a study of millions of people (85 percent from the United States) who voluntarily completed a Web-based version of the Harvard Implicit Associa-tion Test. The study reports: (a) "approximately 68 percent of respondents held pro-White/anti-Black implicit associations, with respondents' magni-tude of bias tending to be medium to large" and (b) "Whites, Hispanics, Asians, and Native Americans, on average, exhibited pro-White/anti-Black implicit associations with a medium to large effect size; Blacks did not show a preference overall" (Warikoo et al., 2016, p. 509). With White educators making up the majority of school teachers, teacher education/preparation programs that embrace the responsibilities of measuring their cohorts' im-plicit associations could (a) develop more useful analyses of racial and class bias as related to novice and veteran teachers' expectations of their students, (b) address the role of teachers in perpetuating racism- and poverty-related inequities in diverse schools, and (c) better prepare teachers to educate di-verse populations of students.

Adults have been conditioned to be more likely to remember and to believe negative stereotypes about people of color and people living in pov-erty (Hilton & von Hippel, 1996). Stereotypes "serve as sort of a glue that sticks separate encounters together in our mind and lead us to then respond more negatively" (Hunt, 2015, p. 1). US audiences are constantly fed dispro-portionate, mass-mediated images of laziness, apathy, and low intelligence with regard to Black, Latino, and impoverished youth and families. Recent studies suggest that such racialized and classed imaging can even negatively influence whether and how educators respond to messages from "Deshawn" versus "David," "Brad" versus "Lamar," or "Rosina versus "Rachel" (Hunt, 2015; Payne, Niemi, & Doris, 2018; Warikoo et al., 2016). In sum, research supports teacher education/preparation programs' making new-normal re-sponsibilities of studying implicit and unacknowledged biases; making vis-ible the invisible. Consequently, teacher educators will be able to support future teachers as they grapple beyond individual bigotry toward illuminating and dismantling the systemic harm of widespread patterns of implicit bias.

Responsibility 3: Reducing Teacher Bias

Teacher education/preparation programs may reimagine their responsibilities to include interventions to reduce teacher bias with both preservice and vete-ran teachers. Programs could adapt strategies identified in the literature on antibias strategies (e.g., Devine et al., 2012). For example, Devine et al. (2012) found that a forty-five-minute interactive presentation describing im-plicit racial associations, the potential consequences of those associations, "and a number of established techniques for improving them (e.g., taking the perspective of stigmatized group members, imagining counter-stereotypic examples) reduced college students' implicit pro-White/anti-Black bias for at least 2 months" (Warikoo et al., 2016, p. 512). In another example, non-Black individuals who centered antibias strategies for approaching a positive, non-prejudiced outcome had better transactions with a Black confederate than non-Black individuals whose communicative behavior centered avoiding a negative, prejudiced outcome (Plant, Devine, & Peruche, 2010). In a third study, Okonofua, Paunesku, and Walton (2016) "demonstrated that simply encouraging teachers to be empathic in disciplining Black students steeply reduced suspension rates" (Warikoo et al., 2016, p. 512). Teacher education/preparation programs may consider implementing similar interventions with cohorts of teachers. For example, teacher educators could engage in studies of other promising approaches, like those antibias strategies emerging from lab-based research that focused upon "changing individuals' mind-sets for thinking about and interacting with minorities" (Warikoo et al., 2016, p. 512). Moreover, cohorts of teachers "could be taught to effectively manage the negative outcomes linked with their racial associations with minimal, but psychologically [and historically] informed, trainings" (Warikoo et al., 2016, p. 512).

The antibias research also provides promising evidence to argue that for teachers learning antibias strategies will require taking the perspective of stigmatized group members. For example, if a cohort of teachers, on average, can learn that families' individual decisions or values tend not to be the principal causes of their present realities (but influenced racist laws related to housing policies, such as redlining, contribute to transgenerational poverty), then it may influence their implicit associations about them (or at least how a cohort of teachers on average acts upon those associations).

CONCLUDING THOUGHTS AND IMPLICATIONS

The research cited in this chapter supports the argument for teacher education/preparation programs' reimagining their preparation of the next generations of teachers. Sticking to the traditional *nuts and bolts* of teaching seems no longer sufficient. In order to dismantle an oppressive system, one must understand it, yet many programs have only one required course on critical pedagogy or social justice in education (Hughes & Berry, 2012). Given our review of studies, it is doubtful that such one-off courses will create the necessary changes to systems, beliefs, and behaviors to thwart the effects of racism and poverty. Teacher education/preparation programs invested in the equity and excellence that so many espouse should be encouraged by this chapter to begin reimaging a program grounded in a structural understanding of racism and poverty. Teachers emerging from such programs will be better prepared to teach students from marginalized communities. Teachers emerging from such reimagined programs would be undoubtedly more aware of the biases they carry into the classroom and can thereby make conscious efforts to mitigate those biases by building healthy relationships with students and developing culturally sustaining school and classroom cultures. Moreover, teachers emerging from the reimagined teacher education/preparation programs will be better equipped to disrupt the harm perpetuated through school systems.

One of the most important skills that teacher education/preparation programs need to develop with novice and veteran teachers is the ability to build upon the knowledge that students bring into classroom, particularly the knowledge that is shaped by their family, community, and racialized, classed, and cultural histories (Hughes, 2003). Yet evidence from research cited in this chapter suggests that teachers' abilities to build upon the knowledge of others necessarily begins with learning and practicing daily the skill of engaging critical self-reflexivity and antibias in order to manage "stereotype-confirming thoughts that pass spontaneously through [their] minds" (Payne, Niemi, & Doris, 2018, n.p.). Tools like autoethnography have been recognized as promising processes for developing the latter skill in teacher education/preparation cohorts, yet such tools remain underused and often devalued by schools and colleges of education (Hughes & Pennington, 2017). Thus, teacher education/preparation programs will need a radical shift to meet more holistically the needs of Black, Latino, Indigenous, and impoverished students. One might anticipate that the next generation of teachers will be better prepared to teach in diverse school settings if teacher education/preparation programs reimagine and deepen their responsibilities for emphasizing a structural analysis of racism and poverty, owning teaching bias, and reducing teacher bias.

REFERENCES

Devine, P. G., Forsher, P. S., Austin, A. J., & Cox, W. (2012). Longterm reduction in implicit race bias: A prejudice habit-breaking intervention. *Journal of Experimental Social Psychology, 48*, 1267–78.

Hilton, J. L., & von Hippel, W. (1996). Stereotypes. *Annual Review of Psychology, 47*, 237–71.

Hughes, S. (2003). How can we prepare teachers to work with culturally diverse students and their families? *Harvard Family Involvement Network of Educators* [blog]. http://www.hfrp.org/family-involvement/.

Hughes, S., & Berry, T. (Eds.). (2012). *The evolving significance of race: Living, learning and teaching.* New York, NY: Peter Lang Publishers.

Hughes, S., & Pennington, J. (2017). *Autoethnography: Process, product and possibility for critical social research.* Thousand Oaks, CA: Sage.

Hunt, J. (2015, April 30). Teachers with subconscious bias punish blacks more severely. *Los Angeles Sentinel.* Retrieved from https://lasentinel.net/teachers-with-subconscious-bias-punish-blacks-more-severely.html.

Kumar, R., Karabenick, S. A., & Burgoon, J. N. (2015). Teachers' implicit attitudes, explicit beliefs, and the mediating role of respect and cultural responsibility on mastery and performance-focused instructional practices. *Journal of Educational Psychology, 107*(2), 533.

Loewus, L. (2017). The nation's teaching force is still mostly white and female. *Education Week.* Retrieved September 4, 2018, from https://www.edweek.org/ew/articles/2017/08/15/the-nations-teaching-force-is-still-mostly.html

National Center for Education Statistics, U.S. Department of Education. (2015). *Digest of education statistics 2013* (NCES 2015011). Washington, DC: Government Printing Office.

Okonofua, J. A., & Eberhardt, J. L. (2015). Two strikes race and the disciplining of young students. *Psychological Science, 26*(5), 617–24.

Okonofua, J. A., Paunesku, D., & Walton, G. M. (2016). Brief intervention to encourage empathic discipline cuts suspension rates in half among adolescents. *Proceedings of the National Academy of Sciences, 113*, 5221–26.

Payne, K., Niemi, L. & Doris, J. M. (2018). How to think about "implicit bias." *Scientific American.* Retrieved September 8, 2018, from https://www.scientificamerican.com/article/how-to-think-about-implicit-bias/.

Plant, E. A., Devine, P. G., & Peruche, M. B. (2010). Routes to positive interracial interactions: Approaching egalitarianism or avoiding prejudice. *Personality and Social Psychology Bulletin, 36*(9), 1135–47.

Skiba, R. J., Horner, R. H., Chung, C. G., Karega Rausch, M., May, S. L., & Tobin, T. (2011). Race is not neutral: A national investigation of African American and Latino disproportionality in school discipline. *School Psychology Review, 40*(1), 85.

van den Bergh, L., Denessen, E., Hornstra, L., Voeten, M., & Holland, R. W. (2010). The implicit prejudiced attitudes of teachers: Relations to teacher expectations and the ethnic achievement gap. *American Educational Research Journal, 47*(2), 497–527.

Warikoo, N., Sinclair, S., Fei, J., & Jacoby-Senghor, D. (2016, December). Examining racial bias in education: A new approach. *Educational Researcher, 45*(9), 508–15.

Part Three

Book Reviews That Contribute to the Dialogue

Chapter Thirteen

What Does It Mean to Be White? Developing White Racial Literacy

Karyn A. Allee-Herndon, Annemarie Kaczmarczyk, and Sherron Roberts

What Does It Mean to Be White? Developing White Racial Literacy
Written by Robin DiAngelo; 318 pages, $40.42, paperback
ISBN 9781433111150; published by Peter Lang, 2012

Robin DiAngelo is a white diversity trainer, social justice educator, and lecturer at the University of Washington. The revised 2016 edition of this book (cited in this chapter) adds two new chapters, including one on DiAngelo's influential concept of white fragility, as well as discussion questions, an index, and a glossary to make the text more accessible both within and outside of academia. The eighteen chapters cover larger concepts like race in education and more discrete concepts of how white people avoid, disengage, and deny racism. The book charges the reader to ask, "What does it mean to be white in a society that proclaims race meaningless yet is deeply divided by race?"

We share DiAngelo's vision of teaching white preservice teachers to recognize the privilege they have over their students of color. Since two of us are white, middle-class women with a background in public, urban, and Title I education who teach preservice teachers at a large public university, we personify DiAngelo's intended audience. While it is appropriate for teachers of color to read this book, white teachers have the most to learn and often operate within a position of power in school communities. "Racism is among the most emotionally and politically charged issues in society" (p. 19), but it is especially important for educators to examine the impact of racism on both our educational system and our students, as well as our role in perpetuating structures that prevent children from reaching their full potential. To that end, we will address the components of DiAngelo's book that most resonate with educators.

The first chapter focuses on race in education. DiAngelo asserts that the vast majority of whites are "racially illiterate" (DiAngelo, 2016), which includes denying both racial inequalities and how we benefit from systemic white supremacy, as well as the discomfort in engaging in authentic dialogue with people of color about these issues. This racial illiteracy restricts our intellectual and emotional growth. If whites cannot explore racial perspectives—ours as well as those of people of color—we will continue to treat our racial perspectives and experiences as universal. Racial illiteracy prevents the building and sustaining of authentic relationships across racial lines. This is especially troublesome given that most in-service and preservice K–12 teachers are white, middle-class women and their public school students increasingly are not. So if white educators are committed to working toward racial justice, we must examine ourselves in the mirror and explore how we can facilitate a classroom community where potentially risky dialogue about racial inequality is supported in a safe space.

DiAngelo refers to frames of reference as well as lenses through which we view the world. Imagine a pair of glasses. These frames are the categories we fit into and might include age, citizenship, gender, religion, class, race, ability, and sexuality. Our frames of reference develop and shift over time and may change based on our experiences. Our lenses are the very personal ways we view society and might include family, place, body type, and experiences. We see the world through these glasses, and unless we consciously unpack our perceptions it is easy to assume that our reality, especially if our reality aligns with white reality, is universal. Teachers should ask themselves the following questions: How have my own cultural glasses shaped how I view others and myself? What might my glasses make it easy for me to see? What might they prevent me from seeing? How might my glasses shape my expectations in life and of my students?

Our frames and lenses can lead to skewed perceptions of the students in today's classrooms. Today's classrooms increasingly contain students of color, but our teachers remain predominantly white. The cultural deficit theory is a common perspective when teachers are asked to explain the challenges faced by students of color. Deficit theory can manifest itself when teachers believe and express that their students do not value education, their students' parents do not care about their children's performance, and that violence at home stresses these students keeps them from focusing in class. Deficit theory is also reflected in the racial disproportionality of special education referrals and exclusionary discipline, lack of access to quality public school resources are ignored, and unequal academic outcomes, which are attributed to children and their families. DiAngelo deftly describes how this type of thinking can segue into danger discourse and other types of racetalk. Teachers often engage in this type of talk about the neighborhoods or communities surrounding schools with high-minority populations. This negative discourse positions, as well as defines, people of color as being dangerous or otherwise less stable, reliable, successful, or safe and thus reinforces the racist system.

This cultural deficit lens, similar to DiAngelo's definition of lenses, stems from implicit bias. In chapter four (Defining Terms), DiAngelo defines implicit bias as the unconscious and automatic prejudice that operates below conscious awareness and without intentional control. Implicit bias is absorbed from the messages surrounding us and results in acts of discrimination. Because implicit bias is below conscious awareness and is often in conflict with what people consciously believe, they are often unaware of the discrimination resulting from it. Actively exploring and challenging implicit biases is a difficult task and can result in feelings of anxiety and vulnerability.

According to DiAngelo's chapter eight ("New" Racism), another significant challenge for white teachers is breaking through the pillars of racism that work hard to keep the status quo in place. DiAngelo frequently refers to the binary perception many of us have that racist = bad and not racist = good. This binary viewpoint makes it very difficult for whites to see the pervasiveness of the system of white supremacy and privilege. Most of us, especially teachers, do not want to perceive ourselves as being bad people. Until we recognize racism as a structure we are all a part of and that whites benefit from, we cannot begin to dismantle it. Throughout the book, DiAngelo discusses other key barriers for whites to actively engage in antiracism, which includes the ideologies of individualism and universalism, racial desegregation, focusing on intent rather than outcomes, colorblindness, and meritocracy. Another major impediment to true understanding is when whites fail to see how feeling shunned or being oppressed in some areas of life do not negate experiencing privilege in others. Indeed, many of the ways white teachers may feel marginalized are, by definition, that much easier to bear *because* they are white.

To be actively engaging in antiracist education, teachers of all races and ethnicities, but especially white teachers, must be vocal allies for students and families of color. We must be willing to be uncomfortable, listen, check our assumptions, take risks, speak up, and teach children about racism. By borrowing DiAngelo's racial literacy framework, we as educators can integrate social justice education within literacy education in our schools.

Reflecting on how our personal frames and lenses, or implicit bias, contributes to systemic inequality can be difficult for many of us, especially if we discover that it affects our classroom environments. It might also be challenging to facilitate racial dialogue with students, although children are often more open and willing to engage than adults. In our current social and political climate, it is vital to begin these conversations to raise racial consciousness and increase racial literacy with our students. The only way to fully validate the experiences of our students of color is to acknowledge the challenges they face by simply being a part of a system designed to oppress them and maintain white privilege. If we, as teachers, truly believe all children can learn and are entitled to the very best opportunities to reach their full potential, we must consider racism as a potential barrier toward reaching this goal for our children of color. "White ignorance is not born of innocence, is not benign and is not simply a matter of not knowing. White ignorance is highly effective at protecting our investments in racism and thus, actively maintained in the society at large" (p. 258).

Chapter Fourteen

Crafting Culturally Efficacious Teacher Preparation and Pedagogies

Rebecca Morris

Crafting Culturally Efficacious Teacher Preparation and Pedagogies
Written by Belinda Bustos Flores, Lorena Claeys, and Conra D. Gist; 159
pages, $90.00, hardback
ISBN 9781498545389; published by Lexington Books, 2018

Due to the imminent need for culturally aware teachers in today's diverse classroom, we partnered to present the essential idea of preparing culturally efficacious teachers in K–12 teacher preparation programs. The idea to write this book came from our extensive work with the Accelerated Teacher Education Program housed at the University of Texas at San Antonio, where creating critically conscious teachers is at the center of the pedagogy. The book's foreword states that today's teachers are teaching "a growing number of students who are racially, culturally, and linguistically different from themselves" (p. vii). As of 2014, K–12 schools served 4.6 million English language learners and the teaching force continues to remain predominantly white, monolingual, native English speakers.

In chapters three through six, the authors document four case studies from educators committed to social justice and equitable education for all students. Flores, Claeys, and Gist follow a research-based model to showcase the need for a more diverse pool of educators, as well as a need for all educators to be prepared to teach a diverse population of students in their teacher preparation programs. The four case studies are exemplars of how culturally efficacious teaching looks.

In chapter one, Creating Spaces for Culturally Efficacious Pedagogies, Flores, Claeys, and Gist introduce the creation of the culturally efficacious evolution model (CEEM) created by the Academy for Teacher Excellence (ATE) at the University of Texas at San Antonio (UTSA). The authors present the rationale for this model through literature grounded in critically responsive practices and democratic principles for a social justice pedagogy. The CEEM uses a socioconstructivist transformative framework made up of five dimensions: awakening critical and cultural consciousness, acquiring cultural competence, developing cultural proficiency, actualizing cultural and critical responsivity, and realizing cultural efficaciousness. In the final stage, teachers become change agents.

The culturally efficacious observation protocol (CEOP) was created to assess classroom dynamics and assist educators in the CEEM journey. The CEOP is made up of nine evaluative strands that assess teachers' development in becoming a more culturally efficacious teacher: developing a consciousness of differences; understanding ethnic identity development, building interpersonal relationships, creating conditions for language learning, expanding knowledge acquisition, advancing self-regulated learning, developing critical reasoning skills, informing practices and encouraging student self-evaluation, and ethical and enduring professional responsibilities.

Chapter two, Contextualizing Culturally Efficacious Teacher Preparation: The Accelerated Teacher Education Program, sets the stage for the need of high-quality mentoring in critical teaching shortage areas, English as a second language being one of many crucial need areas on the list (p. 15). The setting for this case study was purposefully selected to represent the contrast between the culture of the teacher preparation program and the culture of the site where case-study participants were employed in the San Antonio area. The accelerated teacher education program (ATEP) was designed to meet "the need for ethnic representation and in an effort to address the local needs of school districts" (p. 19). The ATEP program required recruitment, preparation, transition, and induction by highly qualified mentors. The ATEP project used a holistic approach to the personal and professional development of selected teachers. Induction, in addition to preparation within the program, was found to support higher retention in high-needs schools and teachers becoming culturally efficacious. Chapter two ends by describing the multiple case-study methodology implemented "to document how critical teacher development is fostered through the CEEM and enhanced through the CEOP" (p. 24).

Chapters three through six pair the case studies with the nine CEOP strands of diversity, identity, social interaction, language, culturally inclusive content, culturally safe classroom context, instructional practices, assessment, and ethical and enduring professional responsibilities. The four case studies detail examples of teachers who use a culturally sustaining and social justice pedagogy within their praxis. Tania, Leo, Catherine, and Kennu are the culturally efficacious teachers examined in the case studies. Proof of their cultural efficaciousness is unpacked within the nine dimensions of the CEOP. The chapters begin with personal background about the teachers and what life events led them to the ATEP program; they end with examples of the obstacles they overcame and the expectations they established to be labeled culturally efficacious classroom teachers within the nine dimensions of the CEOP.

Chapter three shares Tania's story and her journey as a change agent seeking social justice, where all students are treated with respect and are provided with equal learning opportunities. Tania immigrated from Mexico to Texas at the age of 15, not able to utter a word of English. Her experiences of poverty, language barriers, and lack of citizenship help her to relate to students in similar situations. She employs a humanistic approach to teaching that focuses on valuing students and building on their assets.

Chapter four shares Leo's case study, which disrupts hegemonic discourse. Leo is Mexican American and was raised in a transnational world, traveling back and forth between south-central Texas and Mexico, requiring that he navigate two countries. He was raised by his mom and grandmother and grew up very poor. Leo is a special-education middle school math teacher. His passion is in helping Latino children feel connected to the school setting and finding a sense of belonging to deter gravitation toward gangs and drugs. He recognizes that engaging students prevents failure in school and that the goal of classroom teachers should be to be culturally aware of the students in their school culture. Leo is changing the thinking that surrounds "at-risk" students with his passion and commitment towards educational equity.

Chapter five describes Catherine, is a white woman with a doctorate in neuroscience from the University of California. As a researcher, she felt unfulfilled in her career path. She soon realized her calling was teaching secondary biology and chemistry. Catherine believed that intelligence was malleable. She used humor to connect with students and promote language acquisition. Catherine also promotes emotional support coupled with a positive climate to create success for at-risk students.

Chapter provides the last case study: the story of Kennu, from Nigeria, West Africa. He moved to the United States when he was 21 to become a scientist. Just like Catherine, Kennu is a second-career teacher with a science background, and he feels a male STEM teacher of color can be a positive influence on underrepresented, minority, and low-income youth. At college, Kennu was the only racial minority student in his classes. He has a heightened awareness of cultural difference in the classroom due to his lived experiences. He explores ways to assimilate cultural issues that are relevant to his students in day-to-day instruction.

Tania was a "conduit of change" (p. 43), Leo was "inspirational" and "self-empowered" (p. 63), Catherine demonstrated a "commitment" to teach all learners (pp. 80–81), and Kennu provided a "passion" for equitable opportunities in STEM (p. 95). All four teachers realized that becoming culturally efficacious requires constant critical reflection and transformative action.

Chapter seven, Unpacking and Exploring Cultural Efficaciousness: Evidence across Teacher Case Studies, provides a cross-case analysis to detail the similarities and differences between the four case studies. The most observable comparison of all four cases studies is in the diversity strand. All four teachers made connections and reflected on personal experiences that displayed their value in the consciousness of difference. The least observable strand was identity. Leo demonstrated this strand best by recognizing the need to recognize the cultural positioning of students to avoid negative or deficit conclusions about students' actions. Each teacher had areas of strength and weakness, but all four displayed cultural efficaciousness in all nine strands. The chapter ends with limitations within the CEOP, such as the overlapping of strand attributes, capturing more concrete evidence from student-teacher interactions, allowing for greater student voice, and limiting classroom intrusion by the IM.

Chapter eight, Toward Social Justice: Realizing and Sustaining Culturally Efficacious Pedagogies, validates the work of the teachers and researchers in the ATE program. With a "turnstile manner" (p. 122) of teachers leaving hard-to-staff schools, the need to create culturally efficacious teachers who are adequately prepared to teach within diverse populations is increasingly evident. This chapter carried out an inductive analysis of the case study data, which further emphasized the effectiveness of the project. Four overarching culturally sustaining patterns across the participants are innovating and creating a context for all learners, engaging in critical reflexive action, teachers as leaders and advocates, and transporting knowledge and skills across contexts. As success began to emerge in students, the teachers felt empowered to become change agents advocating for social justice. Teacher preparation programs must redesign pedagogy, be culturally sustaining, and encompass a framework that aligns social justice principles with national standards.

The afterword, Final Thoughts: Reimagining Teacher Education as a Commitment to Social Justice, calls for educators "to be unafraid to listen, learn, talk, and work with our communities" (p. 125). Teachers need to truly understand their own identity in order to create change in themselves and their students. This change creates an understanding of injustices and a need to confront them. Finally, teacher preparation programs that do not invest in creating culturally efficacious pedagogy continue to "perpetuate the social structures and cycles that currently exist" (p. 127).

As an educator preparing preservice teachers and a classroom teacher of twenty years, I understand the imminent need to craft culturally efficacious teachers. I agree that the pedagogy must align with the context of the community to sustain student success as well as teacher retention. This book affirms this when it states that "you cannot teach what you do not know" (p. 114). This is also true for students. Teachers must make learning meaningful and relevant to students.

Crafting Culturally Efficacious Teacher Preparation and Pedagogies to show how teacher preparation programs can align culturally sustaining pedagogy with national standards to create culturally efficacious teachers who rally for social justice education with democratic principles. It is also a guide for culturally sustaining pedagogy within the professional development for post—teacher preparation teachers. All educators would benefit from reading this book, and I have strengthened my desire to ensure that I am a culturally efficacious classroom teacher, advocating for change and social justice for all students. I believe teacher preparation programs would benefit from more explicit examples of how the Academy for Teacher Excellence prepared teachers within their program to be more culturally efficacious. Little detail is given about the actual design of the program. We are only told the pedagogical strands. Overall, I feel this is a must-read so all teachers and teacher educators can see the transformative change that can develop when they engage in the nine strands of culturally efficacious pedagogy and create a safe space for diversity.

About the Editor and Contributors

Patrick M. Jenlink is Regents Professor, the E. J. Campbell Endowed Chair: Professor of Educational Leadership, professor of doctoral studies, and coordinator of the doctoral program in the Department of Secondary Education and Educational Leadership at Stephen F. Austin State University. His experience includes classroom teacher, K–12 counselor, building administrator, and school district superintendent. Dr. Jenlink's teaching emphasis in doctoral studies at Stephen F. Austin State University includes courses in ethics and philosophy of leadership and scholar–practitioner models of leadership. His research interests include identity politics, democratic education and leadership, and social injustice in educational settings. In particular, the focus on injustice animates his philosophical position on social justice leadership, acknowledging that in the absence of a socially just practice, injustices persist to the detriment of democratic society. Currently Dr. Jenlink serves as editor of *Scholar-Practitioner Quarterly*, a refereed journal. Books published include *Teacher Identity and the Struggle for Recognition: Contemporary Discourses for a Changing World*; *Equity Issues for Today's Educational Leaders: Meeting the Challenge of Creating Equitable Schools for All*; and *Dewey's Democracy and Education Revisited: Contemporary Discourses for Democratic Education and Leadership*, all published by Rowman & Littlefield. Dr. Jenlink's current book projects include *Ethics and the Educational Leader: A Casebook of Ethical Dilemmas* (forthcoming from Rowman & Littlefield).

Karyn Allee-Herndon is a doctoral candidate at the University of Central Florida, with a research focus on instructional strategies to reduce achievement gaps and how poverty affects cognitive development, executive function, and self-regulation as predictors of school achievement. Ms. Allee-Herndon's responsibilities include teaching undergraduate courses and supervising elementary education interns. Her professional experiences include teaching at high-need schools, working in a large urban district as a coach and PD facilitator, and serving three education companies to facilitate customized PD, support large-scale district implementations and school improvement efforts, evaluate programs, and develop early childhood curriculum. She can be reached via e-mail at: Karyn.Allee-Herndon@ucf.edu.

Adam Julian Alvarez is assistant professor of urban education in the Department of Language, Literacy, and Sociocultural Education at Rowan University. His research investigates issues related to urban education and sociological factors that influence inequity. Appearing in *Theory into Practice*, *Equity and Excellence in Education*, and *Teaching Education*, his scholarship discusses how to support both preservice and in-service teachers in building instructional practices that center race, equity, and justice. He can be reached via e-mail at aja49@pitt.edu.

Ronda Taylor Bullock earned her doctorate at UNC–Chapel Hill in policy, leadership, and school improvement. Her research interests include critical race theory, whiteness studies, white children's racial identity construction, and antiracism. She is the cofounder and director of "we are (working to extend antiracist education)." As an affiliate of Duke University's Samuel DuBois Cook Center on Social Equity, "we are" works to equip students, parents, and educators with the knowledge and skills necessary to understand the complexity of racism and to further antiracist practices, with the ultimate goal of dismantling systemic racism in education and beyond. Dr. Bullock taught English for almost ten years at Hillside High School in Durham, North Carolina, where she resides with her husband, Dr. Daniel Kelvin Bullock, and two children. She can be reached via e-mail at ronda.bullock@duke.edu.

Danné E. Davis, PhD, is associate professor of elementary education at Montclair State University, New Jersey. She is committed to preparing teacher candidates to be effective classroom teachers of all schoolchildren. Dr. Davis has published and presented various papers about diversity in teacher education. In 2017, she designed Haiti and Her People—a website that hosts "a curriculum unit celebrating the heritage and culture of a people" (https://www.haitiandherpeople.org/). Currently, Dr. Davis is exploring the use of LGBTQ children's literature to inform elementary teacher candidates' responsiveness to LGBTQ diversity. She can be reached via e-mail at davisd@mail.montclair.edu.

JoAnne Ferrara is associate dean of undergraduate teacher education at Manhattanville College in Purchase, New York, and a full professor in the Department of Curriculum and Instruction. She is also the Professional Development School (PDS) liaison to the Thomas A. Edison Community School in Port Chester, New York. In addition to her liaison duties, she oversees the PDS partnership network of schools within Westchester County. JoAnne is the author of *Professional Development Schools: Creative Solutions for Educators*; coauthor of *Whole Child, Whole School: Applying Theory to Practice in a Community School* and *Changing Suburbs, Changing Students: Helping School Leaders Face the Challenges*; coeditor of *Creating Visions for University-School Partnerships* (Professional Development Schools Research book, volume 5), and series editor for Professional Development Research book series. Her research interests include professional development schools, community schools, and educator preparation. She can be reached via e-mail at Joanne.ferrara@mville.edu.

Jon Hale is associate professor of educational history at the University of South Carolina. His research focuses on the history of student and teacher activism, grassroots educational programs, and segregated high schools during the civil rights movement. His award-winning book, *The Freedom Schools: A History of Student Activists on the Frontlines of the Mississippi Civil Rights Movement* (2016), examines the role of student activism in the Mississippi Freedom Schools. He is a coeditor of *The Freedom School Newspapers: Writings, Essays and Reports from Student Activists During the Civil Rights Movement*. Dr. Hale's service is grounded in civil rights education initiatives connected to Quality Education as a Constitutional Right, the Children's Defense Fund Freedom Schools, and the Southern Initiative of the Algebra Project. Dr. Hale is the executive director of the Charleston Freedom School and a codirector of the Quality Education Project. He can be reached via e-mail at jnhale@mailbox.sc.edu.

J. Amos Hatch is professor emeritus in the Department of Theory and Practice in Teacher Education at the University of Tennessee. He recently retired after almost fifty years in the field of education. During his career, he published seven books, wrote more than 120 articles and book chapters, was executive editor of two important professional journals, and was named to the editorial boards of several more. His most recent book is *Reclaiming the Teaching Profession: Transforming the Dialogue on Public Education*. He can be reached via e-mail at ahatch@utk.edu.

Sherick Hughes, PhD, is professor of education at the University of North Carolina–Chapel Hill. He is the founder/director of the Interpretive Research Suite and Bruce A. Carter Qualitative Lab, and founder/codirector of the Graduate Certificate in Qualitative Studies. His scholarship centers: (a) critical race studies and black education, (b) social context of education, (c) qualitative/mixed methodology in education, and (d) interdisciplinary foundations of education. Hughes has more than fifty peer-reviewed publications, including two books selected for AESA Critics' Choice awards (2007, 2014). He is the lead author of the new textbook *Autoethnography: Process, Product & Possibility* and the 2016 recipient of a Distinguished Scholar Award from the American Educational Research Association. He can be reached via e-mail at shughes@email.unc.edu.

Laveria F. Hutchison is associate professor in the Department of Curriculum and Instruction at the University of Houston. She is the author of more than thirty-five journal articles and textbook chapters and has presented her work at national and international conferences such as the International Literacy Association, the Association for Teacher Educators, the American Educational Research Association, and the World Congress Meetings in Scotland, Germany, and Hungary. She was invited by the congressional black caucus of the United States Congress to present a speech on the current trends of STEM education. Dr. Hutchison has been awarded more than $3 million in grants from the National Science Foundation and the US Department of Education. Her research interests include the investigation of instructional strategies to enhance literacy achievement and practices that enhance parental involvement among early learners that relate to closing the opportunity gap in STEM education. She is an active member in several professional organizations and serves on the research committee and the NASA STEM

Commission of the Association of Teacher Educators. She can be reached via e-mail at lhutchison@uh.edu.

Annemarie Kaczmarczyk recently earned her PhD from the University of Central Florida (UCF) and is a visiting lecturer with the Department of Clinical and Field Experiences in the College of Community Innovation and Education at UCF. She is a former Orange County public school teacher who taught kindergarten and second grade in a Title I school, and she was named Teacher of the Year for 2014–2015. She teaches courses at the collegiate level that focus on teaching strategies and classroom management, with an emphasis on culturally responsive techniques. Annemarie's research is in teacher preparation for diverse student populations. She is an intern coordinator tasked with observing and evaluation UCF's preservice teachers. She can be reached via e-mail at Annemarie.Kaczmarczyk@ucf.edu.

Sherron Killingsworth Roberts is a professor of language arts and literacy at the University of Central Florida. She has been published in *Reading Teacher, Journal of Teacher Education, Journal of Research in Childhood Education, Journal of Adult and Adolescent Literacy, Journal of Poetry Therapy*, and *Reading Horizons*, among others, and she was a coeditor of *Literacy Research and Instruction*. Her research considers literacy as social practice, the content analyses of children's literature, and innovative pedagogy in teacher education, such as technological applications, literature study groups, and writing circles. She continues to explore the uses of poetry as a reservoir for qualitative analyses, for therapy, and for creating a peaceful classroom. Roberts is a published poet, with poems published in academic journals such as *The Reading Teacher* and *Language Arts*. She can be reached via e-mail at Sherron.Roberts@ucf.edu.

Rebecca Morris is an educator focused on equitable education for all students. Her undergraduate degree in reading is from East Texas Baptist University, and her graduate degree in curriculum and instruction is from the University of Texas at Tyler. She is second-year doctoral student in educational leadership with a specialization in curriculum at Stephen F. Austin State University. She has dedicated twenty years to elementary and middle school education, beginning teaching in a multigrade classroom at Colquitt Christian Academy, where she was later principal and curriculum coordinator. She teaches fourth-grade reading at Elysian Fields Elementary and educational psychology and an early foundation course for the global teacher education preparation program at LeTourneau University. Her research interests include literacy, reaching and teaching students in poverty, mentoring of novice teachers, and community building in online programs. She can be reached via e-mail at becca.morris75@yahoo.com.

Kerron Norman is the former vice president of community-based programs and chief program officer for ANDRUS. After joining ANDRUS in 2012, Kerron played an instrumental role in developing public-private partnerships for providing trauma-informed professional development in Westchester public schools. She also expanded ANDRUS's school-based mental health program incorporating evidence-informed treatment and parent and community education using the Sanctuary Model. She can be reached via e-mail at knorman@lssny.org.

Carrie Robinson, full professor in the Department of Educational Leadership at New Jersey City University, is one of NJCU's institutional representatives to the American Association of College of Teacher Education (AACTE). She has been active in the Association of Teacher Educators (ATE) since in 1989. Dr. Robinson was on ATE's board of directors, was president from 2002 to 2003, and was recognized as a "Distinguished Member" in 2010 at the annual meeting in Chicago. A national reviewer of educational leadership programs, Dr. Robinson served as one of ATE's representatives on the board of examiners for NCATE/CAEP from 1998 to 2014. In February 2018, Dr. Robinson received the Hans Olsen Distinguished Teacher Educator Award at ATE's 2018 annual meeting in Las Vegas, Nevada. Because of her community service on the local level, Dr. Robinson was recognized by the *Staten Island Advance* as a Woman of Achievement in the class of 2015. She can be reached via e-mail at crobinson@njcu.edu.

Eileen Santiago is the former principal of the Thomas A. Edison school in Port Chester, New York. Under her leadership, the school became the first community school in Westchester County, receiving many awards for successfullly educating a high-poverty student body. Eileen is the coauthor of *Whole Child, Whole School: Applying Theory to Practice in a Community School* and copresident of Strategies for Whole Child Education, LLC. Her research interests include community schools, social/emotional learning, and cross-boundary leadership. She may be reached via e-mail at santiagowoodcre@optonline.net.

Daniel Solorzano is professor of social science and comparative education at the University of California–Los Angeles. He is also the inaugural director of the Center for Critical Race Studies in Education at UCLA. His teaching and research interests include critical race theory in education, racial microaggressions, racial microaffirmations, and critical race spatial analysis. Dr. Solorzano has written more than one hundred research articles, book chapters, and research reports on issues related to educational access and equity for underrepresented student populations and communities in the United States. In 2007, Professor Solorzano received the UCLA Distinguished Teacher Award. In 2012, he was presented the American Education Research Association (AERA) Social Justice in Education Award. In 2014, he was elected fellow of the American Education Research Association. In 2017, Solorzano received the inaugural Revolutionary Mentor Award from Critical Educators for Social Justice (CESJ) within the American Educational Research Association (AERA). He can be reached via e-mail at solorzano@gseis.ucla.edu.

Kathryn Strom is assistant professor in the Educational Leadership Department at California State University–East Bay. She teaches courses on working with critical theories and designing qualitative research for social justice. Her research focuses on preparing educators to work for social justice in classrooms and school systems and putting posthuman/neo-materialist theories to work in educational research. Her recent publications include "Non-Linear Negotiations: Hybridity and First-Year Teaching Practice" (*Teacher Education Quarterly*, 2018) and "Clinging to the Edge of Chaos: The Emergence of Novice Teacher Practice" (*Teachers College Record*, 2018). She is also the coauthor of *Becoming-Teacher: A Rhizomatic Look at First-Year Teaching* and coeditor of *Decentering the Researcher in Intimate Scholarship: Critical Posthuman Perspectives in Education* (2018). Dr. Strom is active in a number of professional organizations, including the American Educational Research Association (AERA) and the Carnegie Project on the Educational Doctorate (CPED). She has served as a senior writing fellow with CPED and currently serves as chair of the CPED Social Justice special interest group. She may be reached via e-mail at kathryn.strom2 @csueastbay.edu.

Kelly Wallace returned to the public school classroom as an English language arts teacher at Lenoir City (Tennessee) High School in east Tennessee after finishing her PhD in education. She continues to teach and work on research teams at her alma mater, the University of Tennessee. Combining eleven years of experience in the high school classroom and four years of experience in the university classroom, her focus is on bridging theory and practice for use by everyday teachers in everyday classrooms. She has published a handful of articles and continues to write and present at various conferences. She may be reached via e-mail at kbailes@vols.utk.edu.

Sarah M. Yanosy, LCSW, is the former director of the Sanctuary Institute at ANDRUS in Yonkers, New York. As a clinical practitioner of the Sanctuary Model in her work with children and families, Ms. Yanosy collaborated with Dr. Sandra Bloom and colleagues to create the Sanctuary Institute. In her role as director, Ms. Yanosy has overseen the implementation of this system-wide holistic organizational intervention for more than two hundred organizations, including residential treatment, D&A treatment, domestic violence, and juvenile justice programs in addition to hospital, community-based, and school settings across the United States and in five other countries. She has been a keynote and featured speaker on trauma and organizational culture at both national and international conferences. Her most recent publication is an article coauthored with Landa Harrison titled "Traumatic Reenactment: How This Triangle Can Sabotage Intervention and Treatment," The International Society for Prevention of Child Abuse and Neglect (ISPCAN) (2011). She can be reached via e-mail at Syanosy@gmail.com.

www.ingramcontent.com/pod-product-compliance
Lightning Source LLC
Chambersburg PA
CBHW020356270326
41926CB00007B/458